AMANDA WHITTINGTON

Amanda Whittington is one of the most widely performed playwrights in the UK. Her other plays include *Kiss Me Quickstep*, *The Thrill of Love*, *Amateur Girl*, *Ladies' Day*, *Ladies Down Under*, *The Dug Out*, *Satin 'n' Steel*, *Bollywood Jane*, *The Wills's Girls*, *Miss Johnson* and *Be My Baby*. She adapted *Saturday Night and Sunday Morning*, *My Judy Garland Life* and *Tipping the Velvet* for the stage. Amanda writes regularly for BBC Radio 4, with recent radio plays including *The All Clear* (*Fact to Fiction*) and three series of the Children in Need Woman's Hour drama, *D for Dexter*, which won Best Series/ Serial in the 2016 BBC Audio Drama awards. Her work has become a popular choice for amateur, community and school productions across the country, with *Be My Baby* a GCSE and A-level Theatre Studies text.

Other Titles in this Series

Amanda Whittington

MIGHTY ATOMS

NICK HERN BOOKS

London

www.nickhernbooks.co.uk

A Nick Hern Book

Mighty Atoms first published in Great Britain as a paperback original in 2017 by Nick Hern Books Limited, The Glasshouse, 49a Goldhawk Road, London W12 8QP, in association with Hull Truck Theatre

Mighty Atoms copyright © 2017 Amanda Whittington

Amanda Whittington has asserted her right to be identified as the author of this work

Cover image: Hull Truck Theatre

Designed and typeset by Nick Hern Books, London
Printed in the UK by Mimeo Ltd, Huntingdon, Cambridgeshire PE29 6XX

A CIP catalogue record for this book is available from the British Library

ISBN 978 1 84842 673 3

Mighty Atoms was co-produced by Hull Truck Theatre and Hull UK City of Culture 2017. It was first performed at Hull Truck Theatre on 8 June 2017, with the following cast:

ANETA	Maya Barcot
GRACE	Anna Doolan
TAYLOR	Caitlin Drabble
NORA	Judi Earl
LAUREN	Danielle Henry
BARBARA	Kat Rose Martin
JAZZ	Olivia Sweeney

Director	Mark Babych
Movement Director	Ella Robson Guilfoyle
Set and Costume Designer	Grace Smart
Lighting Designer	Prema Mehta
Composer	Sophie Cotton
Sound	Mathew Clowes
Assistant Director	Maureen Lennon

Producer	Rowan Rutter
Production Manager	Luke Child
Head of Production and Technical	Amy Clarey
Head of Wardrobe	Julia Wilson

Stage Manager	Shona Wright
Deputy Stage Manager	Jane Williamson
Assistant Stage Manager	Vicky Spencer

Boxing Trainers	Matty Davies
	Adam Parnaby
	Seb Glazer
	(Vulcan Boxing Club)

Characters

TAYLOR FLINT, *thirties, female*
LAUREN LEE, *thirties, female*
JAZZ ASHTON, *twenties, female in transition*
ANETA ŚLĄSKA, *forties, female*
GRACE IDLEWELL, *late teens, female*
NORA COOKE, *fifties, female*
BARBARA BUTTRICK, *twenties, female*

We also hear the voice of a FEMALE AMERICAN YOGI,
LADY MP and 'THERESA MAY FROM THE BREWERY'

Setting

Mighty Atoms is set in the function room of The Six Bells,
a run-down 1960s-style inner-city pub in Hull. The ground-floor
room is full of clutter but in the corners are magical traces of
the fairground and circus.

Time

The action takes place in the present.

A Note on Boxing and Movement

Boxing and training sequences may be adapted to match the performers' level of ability. When dialogue refers to specific movements, companies may adapt those lines accordingly. When finding the language of your production, ensure the storytelling aspects of those sequences remain.

This text went to press before the end of rehearsals and so may differ slightly from the play as performed.

ACT ONE

Scene One

Silhouette of a young 1950s woman (BARBARA BUTTRICK),
*shadow-boxing. She is small in stature but what she lacks in
height, she makes up for in skill and guile. Fairground music
blends with the noise of a crowd. The atmosphere is visceral, the
tension high, the sweat and sex of the fairground and the boxing
ring combined.* NORA *takes the role of a fairground barker.*

NORA. Ladies and gentlemen, Bosco's Boxing and Wrestling
Show presents one of the most controversial entertainments
ever to be seen here in Yorkshire. Public interest has been
greatly aroused by the appearance of this brave young girl.
Harsh words have been spoken against her but we know we
cannot condemn without having seen – and you're seeing
her now, my friends! Here at the Hoyland Common Fair it's
our very own battling Barbara Buttrick! The only girl boxer
in Britain!

As BARBARA *deftly moves to the applause of the crowd, we
see another young woman* (TAYLOR FLINT) *watching from
a distance of sixty years.*

Miss Buttrick is eighteen years old and hails from Cottingham,
Hull. Weighs seven stone, stands four-eleven in her ring-shoes
and packs a seven-hundred-pound punch. Makes all her own
gear, including her gumshield, and embroiders her shorts.
She's a shorthand typist and two-fisted fighter who spars with
the lads. And now, friends, she is openly challenging any lass
here up to nine stone in weight.

TAYLOR *is looking from* NORA *to* BARBARA.

Ring clothes supplied and a cash prize for the lass who'll go
six rounds with Battling Butt! She's banned – yes, banned –
by the Variety Artists Federation but she's here now and

throwing a challenge to you, miss? To you? Can you step up to the mark, young lady? Can you take on the Mighty Atom of the Ring?

The cheers of the crowd rise in anticipation. TAYLOR *walks into the centre of the function room.*

Scene Two

Week 1, Monday, present day: The Six Bells function room. TAYLOR *sits, eyes closed, cross-legged and barefoot, on a yoga mat, palms upwards, arms straight, thumb and forefinger making a circle. Her mobile phone plays a Buddhist guided meditation. Ethereal chords wash under the commentary, calmly spoken by a female American* YOGI.

YOGI'S VOICE. Let go... let all return to the source... deep in one's centre, one's core... equilibrium... calm... still...

Outside, we hear the sounds of the estate: kids shouting, dogs barking, a lorry backing up and blokes getting out.

Harmonise with the rhythm of life... the pulse of life...

Enter ANETA *with a mop and bucket. When she sees* TAYLOR, *she turns and clatters out again.*

In rhythm... in peace... the rhythm of the universe...

We hear a bin full of glass bottles tipped into the lorry. TAYLOR *flinches.*

Breathes through the body... one pulse, one rhythm, one breath pulsates...

Enter NORA, *a bunch of keys rattling on a chain.*

NORA. Morning.

Defying an arthritic hip, NORA *walks across the room towards the bar.*

YOGI'S VOICE. Life is breathing... here... now... in this
    body...

NORA. Nor' in this one.

   TAYLOR *bristles but keeps her eyes closed.*

YOGI'S VOICE. Do nothing... let it be...

   NORA *sings 'Let It Be' as she looks behind the bar.*

   Just... Be... Sit... Be still... where the life... the truth... is.

NORA. Here she is.

   NORA *pulls a plastic skeleton from the junk. She moves out
   from the bar humming 'Nellie Murphy'.* TAYLOR *opens her
   eyes and turns off the meditation.*

TAYLOR. What y'doing?

NORA. What are you?

TAYLOR. It's not Halloween till November.

   NORA *shakes the skeleton out.*

NORA. Weight Watchers, in't it, tonight? Might hang her up.
    Motivation.

TAYLOR. You're mad.

   NORA *chants a skipping rhyme as she moves the skeleton
   across the room.*

NORA. Nellie Murphy's got no drawers,
    Won't you kindly lend her yours?

TAYLOR. Do you mind?

NORA. It's working, then? Your inner-peace thing, your 'do
    nothing' stuff.

TAYLOR. It was.

NORA. You'd better get back to it, then.

   NORA *hangs the skeleton on a nail in the wall as the
   ringtone-from-hell starts up.*

TAYLOR. Who's that?

NORA *glances at the caller display.*

NORA. Theresa May from the brewery.

TAYLOR. Well, get it.

NORA. I'm busy. I'm out.

TAYLOR. You're never out.

NORA *rejects the call.*

NORA. And I'm not gettin' talked into buying the latest computerised summat-and-nowt. Wi' music and games and quizzes and bingo and karaoke, all-in-one for six grand. 'It pays for itself when you're not hiring in' but I've told her 'I don't.'

TAYLOR. I know.

Enter ANETA, *with mop and bucket.*

ANETA. Are you done?

NORA. 'I'm the DJ and bingo and karaoke.'

TAYLOR. And I'm off for a run.

ANETA. Where today?

TAYLOR. Spurn Point an' then off the end.

NORA. 'I get my pub quiz for free, online and I'm on the Facebook.' So I'm notta dinosaur neither.

NORA *brings an old canvas sack from the junk.* ANETA *starts to clean the floor.*

ANETA. I cannot run for the bus.

NORA. Then she starts mouthing on about margins and profits and financial planning, and I'm thinking 'tell me about it'. Beer duty, business rates: profits go down but rates stay as they are cos you're valued on turnover, see? Aneta?

ANETA. Yes, I see. (*She doesn't.*)

NORA. And then when turnover don't turn no more – when you're paying out more than you're taking and no-buddy lends you a dime – when insurance has gone through the 'ole in the roof or your boiler's on blink –

ANETA. You mean broken?

TAYLOR. Knackered.

NORA. What do you do? Call Eddie, who'll fix it for pints.

ANETA. Yes but, Nora, you give him the alcohol *after* the job, not before.

TAYLOR. Slam-dunk.

NORA. Cos that's what we do here, that's what she don't understand. We're not just a pub, we're an 'ub. The Six Bells: a community 'ub.

ANETA. With no heating.

NORA. It's June.

ANETA. No hot water to clean up –

NORA. Wi' Weight Watchers, Friday Friends, Knitting-and-Nattering, Alpha.

ANETA. What's Alpha?

NORA. You know, the 'get to know God' thing.

ANETA. In here?

NORA. They can't do it in church, no one goes.

TAYLOR. Best dig out your habit then, ey? Reverend Mum.

ANETA. Your worst habit.

NORA. I'll be providing refreshments.

TAYLOR. A Pint an' a Prayer? That's her worst habit right there.

NORA. What? Keeping me business afloat?

TAYLOR. Sailing close to the wind.

NORA. Y'have to when four tins of Tennent's are three pound in Aldi.

ANETA. But don't push the river –

NORA. When every week, fifty pubs shut down cross country. Not fifty a year: a week.

ANETA. Don't push the river, it flows by itself.

NORA. It does if we all pull together. If everyone round here steps up to the mark and does summat for somebody else.

TAYLOR. Yes, you've said.

NORA. Cos nobody's gonna come down no more sayin', 'Here y'are, people: a blank cheque to build you a centre in place of the one what burned down. Oh, and here's all the classes and clubs to go in. Here's money for Baby Gym, Bums and Tums. Boxercise.'

ANETA. Boxercise?

NORA. Big now, in't it?

TAYLOR. Not here.

NORA. No? It's good for the body, the mind –

TAYLOR. And I've told yer, you've not got the gear.

NORA. I've not gotta bingo machine. Ping-pong balls, cardboard box: packs the place out.

ANETA. Tomato ketchup: that cleans the copper and brass.

TAYLOR. You need stuff, proper stuff.

ANETA. Like…

TAYLOR. Pads and gloves for a start.

NORA. Pads and gloves?

   NORA *takes a pair of old worn boxing gloves from the canvas bag.*

TAYLOR. Where d'you get them?

NORA. St Augustine Lads' Club. He's run it for twenty-three years now, Don Shaw.

ANETA. Can I see?

ANETA *takes the gloves.*

NORA. Kept 'em off streets, off drugs, outta jail. Should be knighted, nor' out on his ear.

TAYLOR. Out?

NORA. Can't get the funding and subs aren't enough.

ANETA. That is a tragedy.

NORA. 'Tis. So I says I'll keep some of his gear for him. Keep it warm, know what I'm saying?

TAYLOR. I know what you're doing.

NORA. Just till he sets up again, an' he will. Cos that's Don: three heart attacks, never say die.

ANETA *puts on one of the gloves and cleans it with a cloth from her pocket.*

TAYLOR. For the last time – no.

NORA. Why not?

TAYLOR. We've been through all this.

NORA. A month ago.

TAYLOR. Nowt's changed.

NORA. Course it has, now you're doing yer Yogi Bear thing –

TAYLOR. Read my lips, Nora.

ANETA. They tell a story, you know? The creases, the tears...

NORA. Look, it's a try-out, that's all.

ANETA. They've heart and soul.

NORA. It's a taster.

TAYLOR. What is?

NORA. The class.

TAYLOR. What class?

NORA. Like I said – Women's Boxercise. Starting today.

TAYLOR. Today?

NORA. Ten o'clock. And blimey, it's five-to.

TAYLOR. And who's gonna run it?

NORA. You are.

> ANETA's *mobile phone rings. She juggles with the gloves and the phone.*

ANETA. Oh!

TAYLOR. You've not listened to me. You've not heard a word what I've said for the last –

NORA. I've heard enough of your pulsing and breathing and 'do nothing' stuff.

TAYLOR. It helps.

NORA. What helps is to do *something*, Taylor. Do anything but...

> ANETA *answers the phone.*

ANETA. Hello?

NORA. I've told Lauren to get a few girls in.

TAYLOR. Lauren who?

ANETA. Speaking...

NORA. Just to give 'em a go wi' a pro.

TAYLOR. I'm not a pro.

NORA. You're as good as.

TAYLOR. Nora –

NORA. And you just need reminding.

ANETA. Oh, hello...

TAYLOR. No, no, no, no, no, no, no!

ANETA. Yes...

NORA. So what else are you doing today?

TAYLOR. Gettin' through it, the best way I know.

NORA. Well, you can do that again at eleven.

TAYLOR. You reckon?

ANETA. Okay...

NORA. I won't have you sat on your arse no more, Taylor. Nor' under my roof for nowt.

TAYLOR. I'm not, as it happens. I'm reading and studying yoga, I'm saving to go on a course.

ANETA. I see...

TAYLOR. To learn how to teach it. In Cornwall.

NORA. Cornwall?

TAYLOR. So there's no point in starting up anything here cos I'll not be around to –

NORA. When? When are y'going?

ANETA. I understand.

NORA. Next week, next month?

TAYLOR. Like I said, I'm saving.

ANETA. Right...

NORA. Right. Till then, call it rent.

ANETA. Thank you, bye.

ANETA *ends the call and silence falls.*

NORA. All right, Aneta?

ANETA. Yes, yes, of course. (*She's not.*)

A buzzer rings, loud and insistent.

NORA. That's them. That's me girls.

Exit NORA.

TAYLOR. Not mine.

ANETA. Bad day?

TAYLOR. I've had worse.

ANETA. Bad week, bad month, bad year.

TAYLOR. Tell us about it.

ANETA. Well, first, I go to the doctor. I say I can't sleep, he offers me antidepressants. Then he says, 'I can refer you for counselling.' I say I don't need it, I know what the problem is.

TAYLOR. Look, when I said tell us –

ANETA. Iga. My daughter. She's eighteen. She's clever, she's so many things but I can't… She won't talk to me…

TAYLOR. That's teenagers for yer.

ANETA. She lives in her own world.

TAYLOR. She'll come through it.

ANETA. How? That was the surgery calling. I asked to book her in to speak to someone but she has to do it herself and anyway, waiting list, six months –

TAYLOR. You might as well talk to the wall.

Enter LAUREN, *in full flow on her mobile.*

LAUREN. I've told yer, I'm not going down George Street no more… No… not now, not ever again.

LAUREN *is followed by* NORA, *and behind her* JAZZ, *who lingers in the doorway.*

For what? To get letched at and pawed at in Revolution? To spend cash I've not got and wear shoes I can't walk in wi'out… anyway, gorra go… Boxercise… (*Shouts.*) Boxercise… so I can smack your fat head in, ta'ra.

LAUREN *ends the call.*

Step-sister. Y'all right, Tay?

TAYLOR. All right.

NORA. Remember her now? Lauren Lee.

LAUREN. Oak Tree Primary? I were the one beat y'up on the rec.

TAYLOR. Happy days.

LAUREN. That's me claim-to-fame now, mate. Flooring a champ.

TAYLOR. I'm not.

NORA. Never mind her, where's rest of 'em?

LAUREN. Who's that?

NORA. The great big gang what you told us you're bringing?

LAUREN. Oh yeah, well... Jen's gotta job now, three days a week. Mags's mum's been out on a bender. Dani's youngest, she's just got excluded and our Kelly's lost her phone, so... I did text Yolande but –

NORA. Right, so there's one of you?

LAUREN. Two of us.

NORA. Two?

LAUREN. Come on, mate. Come in.

JAZZ comes tentatively into the room.

NORA. And who's this?

LAUREN. Jazz.

NORA. Jazz?

JAZZ. All right.

LAUREN. You've got yourself rehoused next door, an't yer, Jazz?

JAZZ. From Bridlington.

LAUREN. Lived out in Leeds before that and then Batley and then where were yer?

JAZZ. Huddersfield.

LAUREN. Been around, ey?

JAZZ. Bit, yeah.

LAUREN. Yeah, well, it's lucky for me you've landed up here cos last lot were blasting out grime all time and Jazzy B's as quiet as a mouse.

JAZZ. Yeah.

LAUREN. Too bloody quiet. So I've dragged y'out kickin' and screamin' to get to know folks.

JAZZ. Get fit.

LAUREN. Fighting fit.

NORA. But you know it's girls only, this group?

ANETA. Nora...

NORA. What?

TAYLOR. It's not a group.

LAUREN. Specsavers!

NORA *takes a second look as* JAZZ *takes off her cap.*

NORA. Oh. I see. Well...

JAZZ. S'all right.

NORA. Course it is.

JAZZ. I don't mind.

NORA. Nor do we. Cos we're all-inclusive in here.

LAUREN. All-inclusive?

ANETA. Flights, transfers, three meals a day.

LAUREN. And all the booze you can drink.

NORA. We've a gay night first Thursday of month and it's better than Fuel.

JAZZ. Fuel. Cool.

ANETA. Welcome to Hull.

NORA. Welcome to Boxercise for Beginners.

JAZZ. Can I just... ask, like... how much it's...

NORA. Three pound a pop.

JAZZ. Three... right...

NORA. Y'unwaged?

JAZZ. Yeah, at the minute.

NORA. Two-fifty to you, then.

LAUREN. Single mum?

ANETA. Staff discount?

NORA. All right, two pound all round and soft drinks half-price at the bar. Have fun.

NORA moves to go.

TAYLOR. Nora, I've nothing prepared.

NORA. You get lemons, you make lemonade.

LAUREN. Who are you calling a lemon?

NORA. There's two of 'em, ready and willing.

ANETA. Three. I think. Me.

NORA. That's the spirit! Take off your tabard, gal. Seize the day!

As the three prepare for the class, BARBARA BUTTRICK *enters the space. She carries an old football and a long string net.*

LAUREN. Right, just to say, Tay, I've got childcare till twelve and I wanna stone off by Christmas.

BARBARA is only visible to TAYLOR, *who watches her keenly.*

Tay?

TAYLOR. Right. Fine. Er... Yo-Bo.

ANETA. Yo-Bo?

TAYLOR. Yoga-Boxing. Yeah. Ying-yang.

LAUREN. Ying-what?

TAYLOR. Complementary opposites: dark an' light, fire an' water. Female an' male.

LAUREN. Yo-Bo, Jazz.

TAYLOR. Shoes off.

NORA. Just go wi' it, girls. It's a warm-up. It's free.

LAUREN. Free?

TAYLOR. Stand up. Tall. Back straight, that's it. Hands together. Palms upwards, thumbs tight to the chest and say after me... Namaste.

LAUREN. Say?

JAZZ. Nama...

TAYLOR. I bow to the divine in you.

TAYLOR *bows to the class.*

LAUREN. Look, if any of this is religious...

TAYLOR *gives her a 'don't mess with me' look.* BARBARA *sets about tying the football in the bag.*

ALL. Numrestre.

Scene Three

Continuous. TAYLOR *leads a Yo-Bo routine which blends movement from the two disciplines. She executes it with grace and skill; her class, less so. Each are ill at ease with their bodies. It's as if acrobats, clowns and elephants are in the circus ring together.*

Simultaneously, and in her own reality, BARBARA *makes a punchbag with the football and bag. She searches the room for the right place to hang it and spots a nail at a high spot on the wall.*

As BARBARA *hangs up the punchbag,* TAYLOR *stops the class with a cursory bow.*

TAYLOR. Namaste.

ALL. Numustare…

TAYLOR. That's it, you're done.

LAUREN. Already?

TAYLOR. Ta.

   Exit TAYLOR, *watched by* BARBARA.

ANETA. Well… that was…

JAZZ. All right, yeah.

LAUREN. Short.

ANETA. Short but sweet.

LAUREN. I came here to burn off the sweet, mate. I came here to shift this, you get me?

   LAUREN *slaps her stomach.*

ANETA. Lie in a hot bath, you'll lose a biscuit.

LAUREN. You what?

ANETA. Have a hot bath and one hundred calories burn.

LAUREN. As if!

ANETA. It's true.

JAZZ. 'Tis. Were on radio, weren't it? This morning.

ANETA. And you exhale one pound a night when you sleep.

LAUREN. Do what?

ANETA. You actually lose a pound in weight every night, breathing out.

LAUREN. Do you bollocks.

JAZZ. In moisture.

ANETA. You do.

LAUREN. How much do you lose in a fart? Cos I cracked a few with that bendin' and –

JAZZ. But then you put it back on, breathing in.

ANETA. Such is life.

JAZZ. Ying an' yang.

LAUREN. And how's knowing that meant to 'elp?

ANETA. It expands the mind, I suppose.

LAUREN. I reckon she's losing hers, Taylor.

ANETA. She's doing all right.

LAUREN. But she's not what she was, is she?

ANETA. I didn't know her back then.

JAZZ. Back when?

LAUREN. Back in the time she were...

Enter NORA, *pushing a wicker crate into the room.*
BARBARA *is reading a battered old book:* The Art of
Boxing *by Jimmy White.*

NORA. Coming through!

LAUREN (*to* NORA). You should have a man in for that.

NORA. Sexist.

LAUREN. A cellar-man.

NORA. I am the cellar-man. Chief cook, bottle-washer.

LAUREN. Bouncer, an' all, so I heard: Sat'day night.

NORA. Never ask folk to do what you won't do yourself.

ANETA. Unless it's the function room after the rugby club –

NORA *opens the crate and the girls dig in.*

NORA. Right, girls! Don left this little lot for us. Gloves, pads, face-guards, skipping ropes, medicine balls…

LAUREN *takes the skipping rope out of the basket.* JAZZ *hangs back self-consciously, the new kid in class.*

LAUREN. Best fat-burning thing in the world.

JAZZ. You're not fat.

LAUREN *starts to skip.*

LAUREN. See? It's droppin' off us already.

NORA. Down by the river, down by the sea,
Johnny broke a bottle and blamed it on me.

NORA/LAUREN. I told Ma, Ma told Pa,
Johnny gotta spanking, so ha-ha-ha,
How many spankings did Johnny get?

LAUREN. One, two, three, four, five, six…

LAUREN *runs out of steam.*

NORA. Big gang of bains we was, singing that. Back in the day. Old washing line as a rope.

ANETA. No TV, no bath, no shoes on your feet.

NORA. We had shoes. One each.

ANETA. We used to do the Double Dutch. All the girls in the street.

LAUREN. Does make you feel like a kid again.

ANETA. Carefree.

LAUREN. Come on then, Jazz.

LAUREN *offers* JAZZ *the rope*.

JAZZ. You're all right.

LAUREN. Go on, you've six to beat.

JAZZ. Nah...

LAUREN. Take it, you'll thrash us, you will.

JAZZ. I said no.

LAUREN. Whass up?

JAZZ. Nuthin'.

LAUREN. I'm not being funny –

JAZZ. I'm not, I just don't do that sorta...

LAUREN. What sorta?

JAZZ. Weren't me, thass all. As a young 'un, you know... didn't like it, so...

Enter TAYLOR, *purposefully*.

TAYLOR. Where's me phone?

NORA. Have a look at all this.

TAYLOR. Can't, sorry. Gotta call to make.

NORA. Cornwall? Who do you know down there, then?

TAYLOR. Excuse me.

TAYLOR *picks up her phone from the floor and turns to go, but* NORA *stops her*.

NORA. We've gear here from Don. They're all over it.

TAYLOR. Course they are, it's the schoolyard all over again.

NORA. And we can build on this, Tay. Get four, five, ten times more girls in.

TAYLOR. We?

NORA. Wi' your skills and knowledge and standing.

TAYLOR. What standing?

NORA. We could have us a Fight Club.

TAYLOR. You train to box, not to fight.

NORA. What's the difference?

TAYLOR. Fighting is physical conflict. Boxing's a sport.

BARBARA (*reads*). 'Fast hands, fast feet and a quick mind.'

NORA. Yeah, a sport for girls now – and they're going to clubs
   where they're trained up from scratch in a couple of months –

TAYLOR. Yes, I know.

NORA. Two months and they're doing it for real in the ring.

LAUREN. Doing what?

TAYLOR. An arm-swinging contest, that's all.

   LAUREN *and* ANETA *are listening now.* TAYLOR *glances
   at* BARBARA, *who puts on makeshift hand-wraps as she
   reads.*

BARBARA (*reads*). 'When your jab is right, the rest of the fight
   will follow.'

NORA. But these clubs, they're setting up everywhere now,
   an't yer seen? They train up the girls for an actual match.
   They raise money for charity, thousands. They take 'em from
   zero to hero.

LAUREN. So, what? It's sorta like *Strictly*?

TAYLOR. It's nothing like *Strictly*.

NORA. The Box-Factor, I like it! We could have posters all
   over th'estate saying –

TAYLOR. How long did it take me? From first time I went to
   the gym to a fight.

BARBARA (*reads*). 'Never shoot for the KO. It'll come if all
   else is right.'

NORA. I can't recall. Three months? Six?

TAYLOR. Two years. Two years of training, non-stop.

LAUREN. Yeah but you was a proper –

TAYLOR. You have to be proper whatever the level. Takes stamina, discipline, courage –

NORA. They've got thar' in spades.

LAUREN. I have, I were married eight years.

ANETA. Twelve.

TAYLOR. So you'd send 'em to fight not knowing who they'll go up against?

NORA. Says on the website they match 'em up: height, weight, the lot.

TAYLOR. Oh, they do. But I could sign up for them classes. Get in the ring wi' an eight-weeker, flatten her.

NORA. But you wouldn't.

TAYLOR. I wouldn't, but others would.

BARBARA (*reads*). 'Speed is king.'

TAYLOR. Them who don't care it's a dog-fight when one random shot to the head can... one shot...

BARBARA (*reads*). 'Confidence... Balance... Accuracy...'

TAYLOR. You don't know what you're on about. None of you.

TAYLOR *puts the stuff back into the crate.*

LAUREN. I'm not looking to win a world title here, mate. I just want rid of me muffin top.

TAYLOR. Weight Watchers.

LAUREN. Bin there, done that.

TAYLOR. Me an' all. So get your stuff, ey? And go home.

NORA. Taylor –

LAUREN. S'all right, Nora. S'all right...

The class gather their stuff as BARBARA *stands at the punchbag and tries to jab. She refers to the pictures in the book as she does.*

BARBARA. You gotta... you gotta... you gotta...

NORA. Refreshments in the bar. On the house.

Exit NORA, *followed by* LAUREN *and* ANETA. JAZZ *turns at the door.*

JAZZ. Bur' is it true? I mean, is it true you were a fighter?

TAYLOR. Boxer.

JAZZ. In the days before girls...

TAYLOR. Girls were doing it long before me. You just never 'eard they were.

JAZZ. True of a lot of things, ey?

TAYLOR. 'Tis. Yeah.

JAZZ watches TAYLOR *for a moment, studying her.* TAYLOR *is watching* BARBARA, *who vocalises her punches with a breath that fills the silence.*

JAZZ. Ta.

Exit JAZZ.

BARBARA *times her punches with spoken lines from the chorus of 'Ac-Cent-Tchu-Ate the Positive' by Bing Crosby and The Andrews Sisters.*

Alone now, TAYLOR *ventures closer to* BARBARA *who is entirely focused on her punchbag. As* TAYLOR *gets closer, she spins around as if to hit her.*

BARBARA. Attack is the best defence, Tay!

TAYLOR *moves back, startled.* BARBARA *carries on with her practice. Then* TAYLOR *hears a voice at the open window.*

GRACE. This it?

TAYLOR *looks up to see* GRACE. *As she comes in through the window,* BARBARA *slows her practice to watch her.*

TAYLOR. What?

GRACE. The thing, the boxing thing?

TAYLOR. What you doing up there?

GRACE. Says it's Mondays –

TAYLOR. Mondays?

GRACE. It says.

TAYLOR. Where?

GRACE. On the poster.

TAYLOR. What poster?

GRACE. On't door of the pub. Boxercise for Beginners.

TAYLOR. Well, if it does, it's coming down. Now.

GRACE. You her? You the…

TAYLOR. Don't matter who I am.

TAYLOR *goes to the door.*

GRACE. You shouldn't do that, you know? Make out you're doing a thing when you're not. You shouldn't Let People Down.

TAYLOR. Has Nora sent you?

GRACE. Don't think so, I'm barred.

TAYLOR. Barred?

GRACE. Yeah.

TAYLOR. How come?

GRACE. For no reason 'xcept for me name.

TAYLOR. Whar' is your name?

GRACE. What's yours?

TAYLOR. Houdini.

GRACE. Who?

TAYLOR. Shut your eyes and you'll see.

> TAYLOR *is aware of* BARBARA *on the periphery of her vision.*

GRACE. Where you going then, ey? To the 'lympics? To win a gold medal? To get rich and famous.

TAYLOR. I'm not.

GRACE. A woman in park says y'are. Saw you running on Sunday. Says to her kid 'Taylor Swift'.

TAYLOR. Flint.

GRACE. See? Y'are. You're her, you're that top woman boxer from here.

TAYLOR. Am I?

GRACE. From th'estate. Oak Tree Lane. Crack Alley.

TAYLOR. That what they call it now, ey?

GRACE. And I googled yer. Saw all about yer.

TAYLOR. Yeah.

GRACE. Everything.

> *Beat.*

TAYLOR. So you'll know I don't do it no more.

> BARBARA *moves between* TAYLOR *and the door.*

GRACE. You still know *how* to do it. You know how to fight girls. They can't take your thoughts out yer head.

TAYLOR. Excuse me.

GRACE. You don't want 'em? Give 'em to me. Go on, give 'em all to me, now.

TAYLOR. What are you talking about?

GRACE. Me cousin. Kira. She's gonna do us.

TAYLOR. Do yer?

GRACE. Cos that's how she is. She said it on Facebook. She's gonna come round and stave me head in and –

TAYLOR. Facebook?

GRACE. And I've gotta be ready. I've gotta be properly ready.

GRACE *raises her fists but only shows her vulnerability.*

TAYLOR. I can't help you wi' that.

GRACE. I can help you, though. Weed, you want weed? I can get what you want in return. I can get anything, me.

TAYLOR. You using an' all?

GRACE. No.

TAYLOR. You better not be.

GRACE. I'm not. I'm fit as fuck, me.

BARBARA. Oi! Language.

GRACE. I'm fit.

GRACE *drops into a squat.*

TAYLOR. Now what you –

GRACE. I am! See? I've watched what you do on YouTube, how you train as a boxer an'...

GRACE *goes into a run of clumsy burpees.*

TAYLOR. All right, all right...

GRACE. I can do it... I can... (*She can't.*)

BARBARA. Show her. Go on.

TAYLOR. It's like this.

TAYLOR *drops into the burpee.* GRACE *and* BARBARA *watch.*

Hands – plank – feet – jump.
Hands – plank – feet – jump.
Hands – plank – feet – jump.

Do it, then.

GRACE *joins in.*

GRACE. Hands… plank…

TAYLOR. Feet… jump…

GRACE. Hands… plank… feet…

TAYLOR. Jump.

GRACE. Hands… plank… feet… jump.

GRACE *mirrors* TAYLOR*'s burpees as best she can.*

TAYLOR. And repeat.

GRACE. See? I can.

GRACE *rolls over in a breathless heap.*

TAYLOR. And now you do it some more. Do it day after day
till you can leg it.

As GRACE *lies back,* BARBARA *returns to her book.*

GRACE. Foook…

TAYLOR. Leg it off the estate as quick as you can.

GRACE. I will but…

TAYLOR. What? What's up?

GRACE. Nowt.

TAYLOR. What?

GRACE. Me inhaler…

TAYLOR. Where?

GRACE. In me bag… quick…

GRACE *is struggling for breath.* TAYLOR *tips out the
contents of her bag: among them a few coins, a keyring,
a pack of ten fags, a lighter, a penknife and a blue inhaler,
which she gives to* GRACE. BARBARA *picks through the
contents of the bag.*

TAYLOR. S'all right, I've gor' it.

GRACE. It's just cos I'm stressed.

TAYLOR. Breathe in, breathe out –

GRACE. Cos of me cousin.

TAYLOR. In rhythm, in peace.

GRACE. What you on about, 'peace'?

TAYLOR. Breathe in… breathe out… in… and… out…

GRACE*'s breathing slows.*

GRACE. I'm all right… I'm nor' having a full-on… it's notta
big thing, I've got an Action Plan.

TAYLOR. Are the fags on your Action Plan, too?

GRACE. They're not mine.

TAYLOR. So how come you stink of it?

GRACE. What, like you stink of bullshit?

TAYLOR *goes to repack* GRACE*'s bag.*

TAYLOR. How old are you?

GRACE. Eighteen.

TAYLOR. Y'at college?

GRACE. Yeah. Sorta.

TAYLOR. Where d'you live?

GRACE. Holly Court.

TAYLOR. Wi' your mum?

TAYLOR *picks up the penknife.*

GRACE. When she's there. (*Gestures to bag.*) Leave that.

TAYLOR. You eaten today?

GRACE. Course I have.

TAYLOR. What?

GRACE. Bag of Quavers. A big 'un.

> TAYLOR *gets a banana from her bag. As she does,* GRACE *picks up the penknife to hide it.*

TAYLOR. Get this down yer.

GRACE. I 'ate fruit.

TAYLOR. I 'ate gobby girls.

> TAYLOR *gives the banana to* GRACE.

GRACE. I'm notta chimp in the zoo.

TAYLOR. Eat.

GRACE. All right!

> GRACE *takes a bite of the banana.*

TAYLOR. And then you can give us the blade.

GRACE. What blade?

TAYLOR. Now who's the bullshitter, ey?

> *Beat.*

GRACE. I'm not gonna use it, am I?

TAYLOR. You don't have to. Y'only need to get stopped with it on yer.

GRACE. I won't.

TAYLOR. You'd go to court just for having it. You'd get a record and then what?

GRACE. Perhaps I've got one already.

TAYLOR. Right, so they'll lock y'up.

GRACE. I can handle that.

TAYLOR. No, you can't.

> TAYLOR *opens her hand for the penknife, which* GRACE *reluctantly give her.*

GRACE. I need it. She's twisted, she's evil.

TAYLOR. Nobody's evil.

GRACE. Kira-Jane is.

TAYLOR. Kira-Jane?

GRACE. Yeah.

TAYLOR. So that means you're…

GRACE. Grace.

> TAYLOR *looks at* GRACE.

TAYLOR. Grace Idlewell.

> GRACE *holds her look.*

GRACE. Taylor Flint.

> *Enter* NORA, *with an orange juice in a glass with a cocktail umbrella in.*

NORA. Them lot insisted on sending this: peace offer…

> NORA *sees* GRACE.

GRACE. What?

NORA. What's she doing here?

> TAYLOR *glances between* GRACE *and* BARBARA, *who has retreated to sit on the crate and watch. She is a shadowy presence as the action unfolds.*

TAYLOR. Who?

NORA. Anne o' Green Gables.

> NORA *is fixed on* GRACE.

GRACE. Nowt.

NORA. Well, then, she can go.

TAYLOR. She's gotta name.

NORA. I know that, gobshite.

GRACE. Grace.

NORA. Idlewell.

GRACE. And who are you, Granny?

NORA. How d'you get in?

GRACE. On me feet and me legs.

NORA. Fine, and you're out on your arse, gal.

GRACE. Why am I?

NORA. You're barred.

GRACE. How can I be? I've not ever been in.

NORA. You're all barred. Your mum, your nan, your ugly
    sisters –

GRACE. They're not –

NORA. That cousin of yours who caused criminal damage to
    my –

GRACE. Not my fault.

NORA. Never is wi' your lot, come on.

    NORA *takes hold of* GRACE *and tries to march her out.*

TAYLOR. Nora –

GRACE. What you doin'?

NORA. Getting rid of the rubbish. Protecting me licence, me
    livelihood.

GRACE. Yeah, like I'm wanting yer livelihood!

TAYLOR. Nora –

NORA. Over and out!

GRACE. No!

GRACE *turns on* NORA *and throws her to the floor.*

NORA. Ah!

TAYLOR. No…

GRACE. It weren't me.

TAYLOR *runs to her aid.*

NORA. See what I mean about her –

GRACE. She did it, she turned an' –

TAYLOR. Don't move now.

NORA. I'm all right.

TAYLOR. Just stay where you –

NORA. Don't make a fuss.

TAYLOR. Is your hip…?

NORA. It's fine.

TAYLOR. How do you know?

TAYLOR *moves to help* NORA *but she resists.*

NORA. No.

GRACE. See? There's nowt wrong with her.

TAYLOR. Shut up.

NORA. It'll take more than her –

TAYLOR. Stop fighting us, will yer?

GRACE. She's putting it on.

NORA *is trying to get up.*

NORA. I'll be putting you on to the police when I'm up on
my feet.

TAYLOR. Steady.

NORA *falls back to the floor.*

GRACE. What's wrong wi' her now?

TAYLOR *glances up at* GRACE.

TAYLOR. Go to the bar out front. Get a brandy.

GRACE. Don't like it.

TAYLOR. Not for you.

NORA. Don't let her loose on –

TAYLOR. Quick as you can.

Exit GRACE.

NORA. She'll have the bottle off and be gone.

TAYLOR. We'll see.

NORA. And if she makes off with a penny of mine –

TAYLOR. Right, so the pub's a community 'ub. 'All-inclusive.'
Unless you're an Idlewell, ey?

NORA. You don't know 'em like I do.

TAYLOR. I know 'em.

NORA. Bringing their smackhead mates on th'estate, drug-
dealing outside my pub.

TAYLOR. I know her.

NORA. Shouting and carrying on day and night: noise-nuisance,
abusing the neighbours, neglecting the kids and I mean proper
neglect...

TAYLOR. I know.

NORA. And we're not going back to that, Tay. D'you hear me?
We're not.

From outside, we hear LAUREN *and* ANETA *shouting.*

ANETA (*off*). Oi, what are you doing?

LAUREN (*off*). Where are you going with that?

Enter GRACE, *quickly, with a bottle of brandy.*

GRACE. Got it.

NORA. See? I told you she'd –

GRACE *shoves the bottle into* NORA*'s hand, as* LAUREN *and* ANETA *come in after her, followed by* JAZZ.

LAUREN. Did you know there's an Idlewell –

ANETA. Helping herself to –

NORA. I knew it, I knew she would –

GRACE. I didn't!

TAYLOR. Shut up and drink.

GRACE *sees* NORA *down the brandy.*

GRACE. Don't thank me, then.

NORA. What, for assaulting us?

GRACE. I was assaulted.

NORA. Whatever. It's done with, so go.

GRACE. No.

LAUREN. You deaf as well as retarded?

GRACE. You're retarded.

ANETA. And let's not resort to those kind of insults. Let's just ask Grace nicely to leave.

GRACE. Why don't you? Back to Poland.

NORA. Now you see why they're barred?

JAZZ. Barred?

GRACE *gestures to* TAYLOR.

GRACE. Why am I barred when she's done loads worse? Taylor Flint. Who makes out she's one thing when really she's –

LAUREN. Taylor's a legend round here. You get that? An absolute legend.

GRACE. All right!

LAUREN. And if you mess with her, then you mess with us and you really don't wanna do that. Do yer?

GRACE. She's a fake.

With this, LAUREN *lunges at* GRACE, *but* TAYLOR *stops her.*

TAYLOR. All right, enough!

The force of TAYLOR*'s response silences the room. As* TAYLOR *looks up, she sees* BARBARA.

BARBARA. Stamina. Discipline. Courage.

TAYLOR. I want tins from the kitchen here now, please.

NORA. Tins?

TAYLOR. And bottles and bags of rice. Ten in all, one for each hand.

ANETA. Sorry, what's…

TAYLOR. Boxercise. Here, now, the four of you.

LAUREN *gestures to* GRACE.

LAUREN. With her?

TAYLOR. The four of you. Now let's see who's faking it. Go!

Scene Four

Monday to Friday. LAUREN, ANETA, JAZZ *and* GRACE *find food tins, bags and bottles in each hand for dumb-bells.*

As TAYLOR *sets up the music, we hear a voice from another time: that of a* LADY MP *from the 1950s.*

LADY MP (*voice-over*). Miss Buttrick is a misguided teenager who's made a foolish, debased choice. Yes, a small section of the sports public may relish the sadistic and grotesque. But would anyone go out with a girl sporting two black eyes? Relish tears from a punch mingled with mascara?

TAYLOR *stands in front of the group, with* BARBARA, *the only one in gloves.* BARBARA *joins the class, although she occupies her own space and time.*

TAYLOR. Ready?

LADY MP (*voice-over*). The danger with Miss Buttrick is that other foolish girls might be encouraged to take up the same.

TAYLOR. Stand wide.

LADY MP (*voice-over*). This is why I call on the British Boxing Board of Control to do everything in its power to prevent the participation of any girls in boxing!

TAYLOR. Straight shots. Go!

LADY MP (*voice-over*). I urge local councils to ban her public appearances! The idea is monstrous, degrading, disgusting, repugnant and wrong!

TAYLOR *calls the routine above the music. They follow* TAYLOR*'s moves, some more athletically than others.*

BARBARA *follows the moves in her own way.*

TAYLOR. Weights under chin, slight squat, keep yer knees soft. Turn your knuckles on top of the move every time... as you come back up, drag the weight back to you an' –

TAYLOR *throws the punches like a pro. Bending both knees in time, the group throw repeated punches with left and right hands.*

Keep breathing: in the nose, out the mouth, in the nose, out the mouth.

LAUREN. In the nose, out the mouth.

TAYLOR. In the nose, out the mouth.

GRACE. Big mouth, big –

LAUREN. You still here?

TAYLOR. That's one-and-two-and-three-and-four, one-and-two-and-three-and-four, one-and-two-and-three-and-four-and star-jumps! Star-jumps!

TAYLOR *leads the group into star-jumps.*

LAUREN. 'Kin 'ell, 'kin 'ell, 'kin 'ell!

TAYLOR. Weights up to shoulder height. Up on the toes, control 'em down. That's it! One-and-two-and-three-and-four-and-jump-jump-jump-jump!

LAUREN. I've got the wrong bra on for this.

TAYLOR. Save your breath.

LAUREN. I've no breath to save.

TAYLOR. Right, let's bring in the legs.

ANETA. Which one?

TAYLOR *leads the group into squats with shots.*

TAYLOR. Arse-down-knee-height. Low squat with a straight shot on the way up, come on! Work it, work it!

GRACE. It's easy, is this?

ANETA. Speak for yourself.

GRACE. Eeeeeeeeeasy!

TAYLOR *starts a military call-and-respond.*

TAYLOR. One mile: no sweat!
Two mile: better yet!
Three mile: gotta run!

Four mile: just for fun.
One mile –

ALL. No sweat!

TAYLOR. Two mile!

ALL. Better yet!

TAYLOR. Three mile!

ALL. Gotta run!

TAYLOR. Four mile!

ALL. Just for fun.

TAYLOR. Uppercut!

TAYLOR *leads the group into squats with uppercut shots with left and right hands. The group lose their timing, rhythm and coordination but they soldier on.*

Turn the knuckles in and away from your face. Punch up and under the chin. Up and under, up and under, up and under. Up and under, up and under, up and under.

LAUREN. And over and out.

LAUREN *sinks to the floor.*

JAZZ. Lauren!

LAUREN. Tell me four lads I loved 'em, all right?

TAYLOR. Keep that squat nice and low. Push up from the heels. Work your glutes. Can you feel 'em in your glutes, Jazz?

JAZZ. Yep!

TAYLOR. Deep breaths now. Deep breaths. Step wide. Squat position. Roll to the right and hook!

Roll to the left and hook!

BARBARA *crosses* TAYLOR*'s vision, throwing a perfect hook.*

Hook, hook, hook, hook, hook, hook, hook, hook! Hook, hook, hook, hook, hook, hook, hook, hook!

JAZZ and GRACE *are just about keeping pace. As they go through the routine, they chant. There is a sense of time passing.*

Day One!

ALL. No sweat!

TAYLOR. Day Two!

ALL. Better yet!

TAYLOR. Day Three!

ALL. Gotta run!

TAYLOR. Day Four!

ALL. Just for fun.

TAYLOR. Day Five!

ALL. Still alive!

LAUREN. Just!

As LAUREN *rejoins the group, the tempo of the workout goes up.*

TAYLOR. Right, let's take it up a gear.

ANETA. I've no gears left.

TAYLOR. Straight shots but faster, come on! Get the shoulders going.

ANETA. Ay-ay-ay...

TAYLOR. Speed! Keep punching! Push-push-push-push-push-and-into-star-jumps!

GRACE. I'm a star! I'm a star!

TAYLOR. Weights at shoulder high. Don't let the weights touch the sides!

LAUREN *is working out with cans of baked beans.*

LAUREN. I'll never eat baked beans again.

TAYLOR. Down to squat. Straight shots. Grace?

GRACE. I am!

TAYLOR. Push from your core.

JAZZ. Push-push-push.

TAYLOR. Jazz! Guard up, elbows tight! Keep punching! Feel that burn in the thighs and keep going, keep pushing. Uppercuts! Arms, shoulders! That's it, keep breathing, keep going, keep working! Yep! Roll to the left and hook, Grace!

GRACE. I am!

NORA *comes in and watches from the sidelines.*

TAYLOR. More power in the punches! Big effort now, all the way to the end! All the way... all the way and... time!

Scene Five

Friday. The group are on the floor now: breathing hard, drinking water, perhaps lying on their backs or with heads in hands. TAYLOR *looks at the room, which is more like a warzone than a workout.* BARBARA *remains onstage, a watchful presence.*

LAUREN. It hurts more than childbirth, does this.

ANETA. Pain is a shadow, cast by a blessing.

JAZZ. Pain is a...?

ANETA. Shadow. Cast by a blessing.

LAUREN. I'm blessed with a banging head.

JAZZ *passes* LAUREN *a can of Coke.*

JAZZ. Drink.

LAUREN. That's yours.

JAZZ. Y'all right, have it.

LAUREN. Ah, you're a good 'un.

JAZZ. Get out.

LAUREN. Y'are.

GRACE. You're summat.

ANETA. Yes, thank you, Grace.

GRACE (*to* JAZZ). What's your name again?

JAZZ. Jazz.

ANETA. Don't you need your inhaler?

GRACE. Your proper name.

JAZZ. Jazz.

GRACE. Jizz.

LAUREN. You'll getta kicking if you carry on –

ANETA. Lauren, don't rise to it.

JAZZ. S'all right.

LAUREN. S'not. It's a safe space, is this.

GRACE. You kick me, I'll floor yer.

LAUREN. Come on then, Klitschko… come on.

TAYLOR. Ey!

Enter NORA, *with a plateful of cake.*

NORA. Left over from Knitters and Natterers.

ANETA. Cake?

LAUREN. What's the point in all this if we have that?

NORA. You've earned it, go on.

NORA offers the plate around.

JAZZ. Ta.

LAUREN. I might take a slice for the kids.

ANETA. And for Iga.

TAYLOR. No, ta.

NORA. So how's tricks?

TAYLOR. Tricky.

GRACE. Totally shit.

NORA. Well, if that's what you think, sling your hook.

GRACE. We're supposed to be learning to fight people.

TAYLOR. Kira-Jane? Who's not been near you since Monday?

GRACE. Well, that's her, innit? All mouth.

NORA. Runs in the family.

GRACE. Least I've gotta family.

TAYLOR. Oi!

NORA. So how come you keep coming back, ey? Five days on the trot? If it's as bad as all that.

GRACE *takes a handful of cake.*

GRACE. Free food.

NORA. Make the most of it. That's your lot. All of yer's.

Beat.

That's it. For now, anyway.

JAZZ. Ey?

ANETA. What is?

LAUREN. What d'you mean?

TAYLOR. Nora?

Beat.

NORA. The boiler.

ANETA. The bane of my life.

TAYLOR. I've told you, just get someone in.

NORA. I have, as it happens. Today.

ANETA. Eddie?

NORA. No.

TAYLOR. Someone proper?

NORA. Oh, this lad were proper, all right. Got all the paperwork, the procedure.

ANETA. So what did he say?

NORA. PCB board I had fitted in April, well, that's on the blink.

GRACE. Boring.

NORA. S'only a small bit of plastic but they charge three hundred quid for a new 'un.

JAZZ. That's a month's money for me.

NORA. Then there's the expansion vessel. Turns out it's full up with water, that's causing a blockage and, long story short: heat exchange.

He's condemned it.

TAYLOR. Condemned?

NORA. Capped it off, shut it down. And shut the pub down in the process.

ANETA. Till it's fixed?

NORA. Replaced.

TAYLOR. Right, so how much will that cost?

NORA. Two thousand pound.

LAUREN/ANETA. How much?

NORA. Once your heat exchange goes, then it's all gone. The whole shooting match.

JAZZ. Two thousand pound…

NORA. It's the labour, the qualified labour. They've gorra be certified, kite-marked, official.

TAYLOR. They shoulda been right from the start.

NORA. Eddie Grant knows his stuff.

LAUREN. Eddie Grant?

TAYLOR. So when you have your hip done, you'll get some bodge-it-and-scarper to –

NORA. He didn't scarper.

LAUREN. Didn't he do...

NORA. He were just sent away for a while.

TAYLOR. Jesus...

NORA. He can't help us. Except with a small bloody miracle.

LAUREN. That really his name? Eddie Grant?

JAZZ, then LAUREN, *sing a couple of lines from the chorus of 'Electric Avenue' by Eddy Grant.*

TAYLOR. Gerra credit card. Nought-per-cent interest.

NORA. I have. I'm maxed out on 'em all.

TAYLOR. Go to the bank.

NORA. They called in the last loan I had.

TAYLOR. Well, you'll just have to get up the floorboards, then. For the stash what you've squirrelled away?

NORA. What stash?

TAYLOR. Cash-in-hand sales, an' all that?

NORA. Cash-in-hand? There it is, that's your lot.

NORA *shows the few coins she has in her pocket.*

TAYLOR. Why didn't you tell us?

NORA. I'm telling you now.

Beat.

TAYLOR. Right, so when I came back... when you said 'have the back room for nowt'... why didn't you say summat then?

NORA. I'm an optimist, aren't I? Glass-half-full, an' all that.

TAYLOR. You're a mug.

NORA. Am I now?

TAYLOR. Running a pub like an open-house-free-for-all:

'Come in, sit by the fire. Well, till the boiler packs up. Stay rent free, till I remember I'm skint.'

NORA. This is not about you.

TAYLOR. No?

NORA. Cos guess what? Not everything is.

The group watches the conflict escalate.

TAYLOR. You shoulda told us to go somewhere else.

NORA. Where? Round the back by the bins?

TAYLOR. I'd have found somewhere.

NORA. Wi' twenny quid to your name?

TAYLOR. Why d'you do it, ey? Why d'you do it, time an' again?

NORA. Cos I know what it is when you're down on your luck; when you're stinking of cider or weed; when you don't speak the language or can't get a job or you're working the system or got put away; when what you're given with one hand gets took with another; when you've got nowhere to go –

TAYLOR. I have – Cornwall.

NORA. For God's sake, there is no Cornwall!

A tense silence falls.

LAUREN. Hashtag awkward.

NORA *looks at* TAYLOR.

NORA. You done?

TAYLOR. For now.

NORA. So as I was saying… two thousand pounds. I need it and fast.

LAUREN. You'll find it.

JAZZ. You'll fundraise, won't yer?

NORA. You can't go out asking for money round here.

LAUREN. They do on Red Nose Day.

NORA. You can't tell folk to sponsor each other or buy tickets for raffles wi' soap-on-a-rope as a prize.

ANETA. But if it's a good cause.

NORA. I'm not going up the precinct to rattle a tin when half of 'em can't pay their gas.

LAUREN. They've money for scratch cards.

NORA. They haven't, they're living in hope.

Beat.

TAYLOR. The brewery…

NORA. Repairs and maintenance, that's down to me.

TAYLOR. Phone her, Theresa May.

NORA. Not with me hand out.

TAYLOR. Tell her, without it you're homeless.

ANETA. Your staff will be jobless.

NORA. She's not gonna help us now, is she? We're up the creek on our own.

LAUREN. What do you want, Nora? What do you need?

NORA. As I said. A small bloody miracle.

BARBARA *moves into the space.*

GRACE. What'd Barbara do?

LAUREN. Barbara who?

GRACE. Buttrick.

ANETA. Does she live round here?

NORA. How do you know about her?

GRACE. I googled her. 'Girls – boxing – Hull'. She come up.

LAUREN. Who is she then?

GRACE. The first World Women's Boxing Champion.

LAUREN. When were that?

NORA. Fifty-seven.

LAUREN. And she comes from…

NORA. Cottingham.

LAUREN. That's not Hull.

NORA. She had to fight in the fairgrounds and carnivals.
    Fought for the right to fight. No one else gave her a shot.

GRACE. And she's me role model now, Tay. Not you.

LAUREN. How come we've not heard of her?

NORA. Y'have now. Mighty Atom, they called her. After
    Jimmy Wilde, World Flyweight Champion. The Mighty
    Atom of the Ring.

GRACE. What is an atom?

ANETA. A minute source of energy.

JAZZ. Nuclear energy.

ANETA. Barbara Buttrick…

LAUREN. By the sound of her, she'd say get out there. Get out
    there and fight for the money. All four of yer. In a Fight Night.

JAZZ. Fight Night?

ANETA. And when you say 'all four'?

LAUREN. Me, you and Jazz, and that one we all wanna punch.

GRACE. Bring it on.

LAUREN. In a charity fundraiser. Save The Six Bells.

NORA. Well?

Beat.

TAYLOR. You're not ready.

LAUREN. We could be. If you...

TAYLOR. Takes two years, I told yer.

LAUREN. Two months, Nora says.

NORA. Two months without takings? Too late.

LAUREN. So how long then, how long have we got?

NORA. Two weeks.

TAYLOR. Can't be done.

BARBARA. They said that to me.

TAYLOR *looks at* BARBARA.

TAYLOR. Why can't you leave me alone?

LAUREN. Cos you're the one with the knowledge, the training, the expertise. You're the one, Tay.

JAZZ. Y'are.

LAUREN. If we put in the hours?

ANETA. Work every day.

JAZZ. All day every day.

GRACE. If you show us prop'ly to...

LAUREN. Strictly Come Boxing, ey?

NORA. Can yer?

BARBARA. Can you step up to the mark?

NORA. Cos without it, we're Don Shaw. Done for.

Beat.

TAYLOR. Exhibition match, you heard of them? Sparring. To show off your skills to your family and friends. (*To* NORA.) Five pound on the door and a cash-in-hand bar...

NORA. And if we packed the place out...

LAUREN. You mean it?

GRACE. You'll actually –

TAYLOR. But no publicity, right? Word-of-mouth, strictly under the radar. Four punches. That's all boxing is. That's all you need to know.

GRACE. What are they?

TAYLOR. Jab, heavy cross, right hook, uppercut.

GRACE. Show us. Show us now.

> GRACE *and the class mirror* TAYLOR*'s moves.* NORA *stands back and watches.*

TAYLOR. Stand left foot forward, bit pigeon-toed.

BARBARA. Right foot shoulder-width behind.

TAYLOR. At a forty-five-degree angle, like this.

GRACE. What's a degree?

TAYLOR. Don't lock your knees, bend 'em. Bend 'em!

GRACE. I am.

TAYLOR. Don't have your feet flat to the floor. Weight evenly distributed – now transfer it.

BARBARA. Foot to foot.

TAYLOR. Keep on your toes.

BARBARA. Left shoulder in, over the foot.

TAYLOR. Upper body to right, makes you a smaller target. Now, put up your fists.

BARBARA. Press elbows to ribs.

TAYLOR. Hands by your chin.

BARBARA. Left in front

TAYLOR. Slightly higher, so you're looking over it, see?

GRACE. Like this?

TAYLOR. That's it!

GRACE. Like this!

> TAYLOR *puts up her gloves and demonstrates a jab. As she does,* BARBARA *shadows her.*

TAYLOR. Jab's your lead-off, your basic punch.

BARBARA. Jab first and rest'll follow.

TAYLOR. Puts your opponent on back foot; sets up your big shots.

BARBARA. It's quick and it's fast and it's – that, see?

TAYLOR. Extend your left arm out front. Step in with your left foot.

BARBARA. Bring your arm back: straight, mind! Don't bend your elbow.

TAYLOR. Wrist firm. Turn your fist at the end, flat to the floor.

BARBARA. Snap it out and back, close to the body.

GRACE. Like this?

> TAYLOR *turns her attention to* GRACE.

TAYLOR. When you box, you're transferring weight body-to-fist, strength-to-power. It's maximum force in minimum time. It's the torque.

GRACE. What's a torque?

TAYLOR. A twist of the hip, the waist, the shoulder, the wrist. And weight backs it up; that's weight as in muscle, not fat so –

LAUREN. I'm gonna be thin as a lat.

ANETA. What is a lat?

JAZZ. It's like a wood thing –

GRACE. Will yer shut up an' listen an' learn!

BARBARA. Four punches, Taylor. That's all.

TAYLOR *turns and she's in* BARBARA*'s reality. She and*
BARBARA *shadow-box together. For the first time, we see*
TAYLOR*'s skill, technique and singular focus. In the*
shadows, the class practise their jabs but we watch TAYLOR
and BARBARA *moving as one. They are street-dance, ballet*
and circus: a thrilling double act. BARBARA *steps back,*
leaving TAYLOR *centre-stage. As* TAYLOR *shadow-boxes,*
the intensity grows. From it comes an anger. The anger rises
to boiling point. It triggers a memory which brings her to a
sharp and sudden stop.

ACT TWO

Scene One

Weeks 2 to 3. GRACE *is alone with a skipping rope. She starts to skip but it's clear she hasn't done it before. She doesn't expect it to be so difficult to coordinate her hands, feet and mind. She repeatedly gets entangled in the rope, but perseveres.*

GRACE. Down by...
    Down by...
    Down by the...
    Down by the...
    Down by...

    GRACE *tussles with the rope, tying herself in knots and making painfully slow progress. She stumbles at every stroke but tries again and again.*

    Down by the river
    Down by the –
    Down by the river
    Down by the –
    Sea!

    Sea... sea... sea...
    Johnny broke a –
    Broke
    Johnny broke a bottle
    And blamed it on...

    Despite her lack of technique, a rhythm starts to build. As it does, BARBARA *comes into view. She jumps inside the rope, skipping with* GRACE.

    Down by the river –

BARBARA. Down by the sea,
    Johnny broke a bottle,
    And blamed it on me.

GRACE finds herself skipping without stumbling. She whoops with joy. As she does, we see JAZZ, watching BARBARA, who motivates her to join in.

I told Ma, Ma told Pa,
Johnny gotta spanking, so ha-ha-ha,
How many spankings did Johnny get?

We see LAUREN and ANETA, skipping in time to GRACE.

They are all sharper and fitter.

ALL. Two, three weeks!

We are now experiencing the routine as they are: hearing the blood pumping through their veins, the intensely felt energy. And at the heart of it all, TAYLOR calls the routine, which may include double-hops, jumping jacks and figure-eights. It ends with ten seconds of speed-skipping.

TAYLOR. Yes... you look beautiful!

A spirit is unleashed. The group whoop and cheer as they come to an end. A fairground flickers at the far edge of their vision.

Scene Two

Week Four. Tuesday. The class finish their daily skipping routine, physically tired but in good spirits. TAYLOR is calling the shots and BARBARA is weaving among them.

TAYLOR. Fast hands! Fast feet! Quick mind! So let's use it, let's work it.

LAUREN. We will in a minute.

TAYLOR. Skills pay the bills but there's one thing you can't fight without and that's...

LAUREN. Sleep.

ANETA. We sleep when we're dead.

LAUREN. I think I am dead.

GRACE. Gloves.

JAZZ. Fists.

ANETA. Brains.

TAYLOR. But what do you need most of all, ey?

LAUREN. Rest.

TAYLOR. The coward runs from it, the fighter, she faces it?

JAZZ. Fear?

TAYLOR. Gor' it in one.

JAZZ. Y'can't be brave without fear, Ali said.

LAUREN. Ali who?

JAZZ. Muhammad.

TAYLOR. So we've gotta find it within ourselves: face it, use it, express it. Prowl like Tyson, rap like Mayweather Junior, shout from the rooftops, yeah? 'I Am the Greatest!'

GRACE. I am!

TAYLOR. Turn the fear around in your head and you make yourself IN-VINC-IBLE. Say it?

GRACE. INVISIBLE!

LAUREN. Invincible, thick-head.

GRACE. Safe space?

TAYLOR. All of yer.

LAUREN/GRACE/JAZZ/ANETA. IN-VINC-IBLE.

TAYLOR. An' again!

LAUREN/GRACE/JAZZ/ANETA. IN-VINC-IBLE.

TAYLOR. An' again!

LAUREN/GRACE/JAZZ/ANETA. IN-VINC-IBLE.

TAYLOR. Now walk round the room like it's yours and yours only, you get me? Own the room! Own it! Walk the floor like you mean it!

As the class walk the floor, BARBARA *joins them, sparring, ducking and diving in her own reality.*

ANETA. I mean it… I really mean it…

TAYLOR. And as you're walking, make eye contact with someone. Tell her it's your place… she's here on your terms.

ANETA. This is my place.

GRACE. You're here on my terms.

TAYLOR. In your own words, ey?

LAUREN. Gerr' out of my pub!

TAYLOR. You're playing at it! Do it!

ANETA. Get out!

LAUREN. Get out!

JAZZ. Get out!

GRACE. GET OUT OF MY FAAAAAAAAAAAACE!!!

LAUREN. All right!!

TAYLOR *channels* BARBARA.

TAYLOR/BARBARA. Accentuate the positive!

JAZZ *channels Muhammad Ali.*

JAZZ. 'I don't have to be what you want me to be.'

TAYLOR/BARBARA. Eliminate the negative!

JAZZ. 'I don't have to be what *you* want me to be.'

LAUREN. Get you, Muhammad Ailment!

TAYLOR. And… rest…

Enter NORA.

NORA. Pasta for lunch in the lounge bar.

GRACE. Love it.

Exit GRACE.

NORA. And off she runs like a spring lamb.

TAYLOR. To the slaughter.

LAUREN. Shame that, when she's almost civilised.

TAYLOR. Small miracles, ey?

ANETA. And here's one more: I've slept through the night for
a week now.

JAZZ. I got up at six and ran eight miles.

LAUREN. And I've been online again.

JAZZ. What happened?

LAUREN. Wouldn't you like to know?

Exit LAUREN, *followed by* JAZZ *and* ANETA.

NORA. They've all knuckled down to it, ey?

TAYLOR. They're having a laugh.

NORA. You an' all, gal. I've seen yer.

TAYLOR. Oh, this Clint Eastwood face never cracks.

NORA. You're not fooling me, Tay. No way.

TAYLOR *picks up a pair of boxing gloves.*

TAYLOR. Sold 'em a pup though, an't I? Pulled off the best
con trick since polling day.

NORA. What?

TAYLOR. Boxing for girls. This thing what's meant to
empower us, whatever that means... but what we proved
with it, what we achieved?

NORA. Progress, in't it?

TAYLOR. But who says it's progress for girls to knock nine shades o' shit out each other? To train for a violent assault –

NORA. That's not what they've come for.

TAYLOR. Grace has.

NORA. They're here cos of you. Cos of who y'are, what y'are, what you achieved.

TAYLOR *drops the boxing gloves into the basket.*
BARBARA *is warming down.*

TAYLOR. Except I weren't good enough in the end.

NORA. For what?

TAYLOR. 2012.

NORA. You were *this* close.

TAYLOR. Weren't fast enough, sharp enough, strong enough – mentally, anyway.

NORA. You were strong enough to pull yourself up and out.

TAYLOR. But...

NORA. What? What now, five years on?

TAYLOR. But if I'd not had the dream in the first place, I'd notta been dropped. And if I'd notta been dropped, I'd notta been drinking, and if I'd notta been drinking...

NORA. How old were you when you knocked on my door?

BARBARA. 1955. Age twenty-five.

NORA. Y'asked for a bed for the night, stayed a year and a half.

BARBARA. One thousand exhibitions with men; eighteen pro fights with women.

NORA. You forget how it was here, back then, the estate. Crime through the roof, folks scared to go out in the day, never mind dark. Lads shooting up in the street, young girls having sex in the stairwells for money.

TAYLOR. Not just young 'uns.

NORA. And you knew very well if you stayed with your ma, you'd end up... You knew at fifteen what to do and you did it, you turned things around.

TAYLOR. I got out. Now I'm back where I started.

NORA. Back home.

TAYLOR. Home...

NORA. Where kids now, they don't need to do what you did. They don't have to leave to achieve cos it's here: opportunity, hope. Cos we fought for the streets to be safer, the shops to stay open, the schools not to sink in the mire.

TAYLOR. You did.

NORA. And we're still fighting, now more than ever.

NORA *sits, wearily. As she does,* BARBARA *begins preparations for a fight. Throughout the scene, she will lace up her boots and limber up. Occasionally, she'll focus on the unfolding events in* TAYLOR*'s reality.*

TAYLOR. Y'all right?

NORA. Yeah, yeah.

TAYLOR. Is it your hip?

NORA. It's always me hip.

TAYLOR. Have you heard from the hospital, have you been given a date?

NORA. I've had three dates for that. Can't fit 'em in, can I?

TAYLOR. 'Fit 'em in'?

NORA. Wi' the pub, wi' all this going on.

TAYLOR. You coulda got someone to cover. I'd cover.

NORA. Oh aye?

TAYLOR. If that's what it takes to get yer... and for God's sake, you're only on crutches. I'd prop you at th' end of the bar.

NORA. Me hip's the least of my worries, Tay.

TAYLOR. Why? What do you mean?

NORA*'s mobile phone rings. She glances at the screen.*

NORA. Theresa.

TAYLOR. You've gotta speak to her some time.

NORA *lets the phone go to voicemail and looks at* TAYLOR.

NORA. We've got four girls here raring to go. And thirty-five tickets sold.

TAYLOR. Thirty-five?

NORA. And I know we'll get walk-ups. We'll sell tins on top –

TAYLOR. Tennent's from Aldi, cash-in-hand.

NORA. Bur' it's not gonna cover it. Not at this rate.

Beat.

TAYLOR. Right, so two hundred people gets us a grand on the door, add your beer sales to that...

NORA. Add you.

TAYLOR. You've got me, I'm here, I've not let you down, I've –

NORA. Add you to the bill. Top of the bill. For a comeback appearance.

TAYLOR. Comeback?

NORA. Cos if word gets out that you're gettin' up there –

TAYLOR. I'm not.

NORA. We'll pack 'em in.

TAYLOR. And they'll pack me off back to...

NORA. You don't have to fight. Just... show 'em you're still here, you've still got the moves.

BARBARA *steps forward, her gloves on but unlaced.*

TAYLOR. You know I can't.

BARBARA. Gloves?

NORA. Can't up here? (*Taps her head.*)

TAYLOR. I'm a has-been, a washed-up... I'd be a freak show now.

BARBARA. Gloves...

> BARBARA *holds her gaze.* TAYLOR *laces her gloves.* NORA *watches her.*

NORA. Well?

BARBARA. You wanna do something? Do it.

NORA. Taylor?

BARBARA. Do it.

TAYLOR (*to* BARBARA). How?

> BARBARA *spins around and into a one-woman sparring match.*

BARBARA. The boys around Jimmy's Gym in Dallas were amazed at the speed! Finesse! Knowledge! Shown by the wisp of a girl – five feet and ninety-five pounds – moving with the rhythm of a ballet dancer – sped through – three – rounds with a-hundred-and-thirty-eight-pound, long-time-professional-fighter, Jose Andres. Jose wasn't trying to get rough – but he could-not-lay-a-glove-on-her.

TAYLOR. Wham-bam-thank-you-ma'am!

NORA. Is that a yes?

> TAYLOR *turns from* BARBARA *to* NORA.

TAYLOR. No.

NORA. Is it a no?

BARBARA. Is it?

TAYLOR. No.

Scene Three

Later that day. Enter LAUREN, JAZZ, ANETA *and* GRACE, *rehydrated and ready to rumble.*

LAUREN. I tell yer, I'm on it. On it like a bloody car bonnet.

JAZZ. Carbuncle.

LAUREN. You what?

JAZZ. Car-buncle.

ANETA. She's joking.

JAZZ. She don't get me, she never does.

LAUREN. Don't wanna get yer.

GRACE. Nor me.

LAUREN. Oi!

LAUREN *takes a playful swipe at* GRACE.

ANETA. So you're on what?

LAUREN. I'm signed up, as of last night. With a profile an' everything.

GRACE. What site?

LAUREN. Like I'm telling you.

ANETA. Are you looking for friendship or…

LAUREN. No ta, I've got too many friends.

GRACE. Well, you'll not get no sex.

LAUREN. Who says I want it?

GRACE. Whar' else are you on for?

LAUREN. I'm dipping a toe in the water, that's all.

GRACE. Filthy water.

LAUREN. You should know.

JAZZ. So what have you called yourself, ey?

LAUREN. La-La, as in Lauren.

JAZZ. La-La, as in Land.

LAUREN. La-La-25. Cos that's me age. Dating age.

GRACE. Plus ten –

LAUREN. Piss off –

GRACE. Stones.

LAUREN. You can't touch me, you know?

GRACE. Don't wanna.

LAUREN. Wi' all your negative thoughts. Cos after three weeks of this, I'm slimmer and fitter and I FEEL GOOD! YOU GET ME, WORLD. GOOOOOOD!

JAZZ. You look good, an' all.

GRACE. I look better.

ANETA. And I say to Iga: 'We can't change the world but if we change how we feel in the world...'

NORA *enters, carrying an old cardboard box marked 'Lost Property' and clanging a bell.*

NORA. Seconds out!

LAUREN. More like bring out your dead.

NORA. What d'you think?

LAUREN. Can't you get one wi' more of a clang?

NORA. 'Tis a clang.

LAUREN. A pub clang.

NORA. It's a ding-dong, what more do you want?

JAZZ. A ding-dong for a ding-dong.

LAUREN. Geek.

NORA. Seconds out – round four!

NORA *rings the bell and* LAUREN *squares up to* JAZZ. *They playfully shadow-box in a Nina Simone pastiche.*

LAUREN. Got me legs, got me fists, got me eyeballs, got me wrists –

JAZZ. Got me knees, got me toes, got me earlobes!

GRACE. Get a room.

LAUREN. Got me nails, got me nips –

JAZZ. Got me knuckles –

LAUREN. Got me lips –

JAZZ. Got me head –

LAUREN. Got me hair –

JAZZ. I got

LAUREN/JAZZ. Life!

GRACE. Can't sing though, can yer?

ANETA. Grace, be nice.

GRACE. I'm not here to be nice.

NORA *is pulling boxing kit from the cardboard box.*

NORA. Right, I've tapped up Don Shaw for your clobber.

LAUREN. Lost property?

NORA. There's boots in here, trunks, mouthguards…

GRACE. From somebody's actual mouth?

LAUREN. Be too small for you, gobshite.

NORA. Breastplates, look. Satin robes.

ANETA *sniffs a robe as the group rifle through the box.*

ANETA. Which hasn't been washed.

NORA. Take it home, give it a rinse-out.

ANETA. A soak. For maybe a week.

NORA. There's no sports bras but I'm sure you'll make arrangements.

JAZZ. And, er, the changing facilities?

NORA. Facilities?

JAZZ. Yeah. I'm just wondering what are they? Where are they?

NORA. In here.

JAZZ. Where?

NORA. Here.

JAZZ. Where the crowd are?

NORA. We'll put up a curtain.

JAZZ. Right, so we're in, like, together?

LAUREN. All for one and one for all.

GRACE. Nor' in these we're not.

> GRACE *holds up a pair of worn-out shorts as* LAUREN *finds a handful of jars in the box.*

NORA. Don says to put Vaseline over your face so the punches slide off.

ANETA. We're in headguards.

NORA. And to rub down the rest of your body with that.

LAUREN. What is it?

NORA. Embrocation.

ANETA. Nice word.

> LAUREN *sniffs the pot.*

LAUREN. Nice pong.

NORA. And he did recommend get a pregnancy test.

ANETA. Excuse me?

NORA. Just to be on the safe side, you know?

LAUREN. I am on the safe side.

ANETA. Very far on the safe side...

JAZZ. It's not an issue.

GRACE. And I'm notta slapper.

LAUREN. Will you shut your potty-mouth now!

GRACE. I'm not.

NORA. Now, nobody's got any medical anything, have they?
Heart, kidneys, waterworks?

GRACE. Asthma.

LAUREN. Yes, we know.

NORA. And if we were doing this prop'ly –

JAZZ. We are.

NORA. Prop'ly-prop'ly, we'd get a doctor in, checking you out.
But in my humble opinion, we don't need to bother with *all*
the formalities…

ANETA. Or a stained 'robe' that some teenage boy's…

JAZZ. His shorts.

GRACE *throws a vest back in the box*.

GRACE. His dirty vest. I'll sort me own stuff, ta.

LAUREN. All the gear, no idea.

NORA. Look, Taylor's got kit here in storage. Good kit from
when she were sponsored.

GRACE. Labels?

LAUREN. Like Nicola Adams good?

NORA. You might get into 'em now you're toned-up.

LAUREN. Oh, ta.

NORA. What I mean is you look the part now, all of yer. You're
fast-on-the-feet, you're quick-in-the-mind. And you're
looking to me like you could push it that little bit more.

ANETA. We're pushing as hard as we can.

NORA. Course y'are. But I'm thinking with all of the effort you're making, perhaps you might wanna think about... now you're so into it...

LAUREN. Think about...

NORA. Raising the bar.

GRACE. That bar? (*Gestures to the actual bar.*)

NORA. No –

LAUREN. Knucklehead.

NORA. The bar of achievement, excellence, competition.

ANETA. What are you trying to say?

NORA *glances to the door and back to the class.*

NORA. Well, we could do a weigh-in on Weight Watchers scales but as you're all roughly the same...

NORA *is sizing them up.*

LAUREN. What?

NORA. Say... Aneta v Grace? And Lauren v Jazz.

GRACE. What's 'vee'?

ANETA. Versus. Against.

GRACE. What? Like an actual fight?

ANETA. We're learning to box.

LAUREN. An actual... box?

NORA. Two rounds, two minutes each. That's what the girls do, I've looked it up.

ANETA. Four minutes.

LAUREN. We're running for thirty.

NORA. And then we, The Six Bells, could run a book, ey? To top up the boiler fund. Hit the target and more.

JAZZ. But Taylor says it's an exhibition match – skills only.

NORA. Never mind her. What do you wanna do? After all your training and learning and running and struggle and sacrifice... what?

JAZZ *looks at* LAUREN.

JAZZ. I couldn't fight Lauren.

LAUREN. You're right. You'd be toast.

JAZZ. You'd be cheese on toast.

LAUREN. Cheddar cheese on toast.

GRACE *looks at* ANETA.

GRACE. I'd like to see you try battering me.

JAZZ. Wi' brown sauce.

ANETA. I'd batter you like a sausage.

LAUREN. Red.

JAZZ. Brown.

LAUREN. Red-brown.

JAZZ. Maroon.

GRACE. Battered hot-dog sausage.

LAUREN. I'd leave you frickin' maroon.

NORA. That's the spirit. That's it!

Exit NORA, *with* GRACE *and* ANETA.

Scene Four

Wednesday. LAUREN *and* JAZZ *are nose-to-nose in a boxing stare-down.*

LAUREN. You ready?

JAZZ. You ready?

LAUREN. You might think you're ready.

JAZZ. You might think you're Eddie.

LAUREN. Stop it...

JAZZ. You might think you're gonna...

> LAUREN *picks up the lines of 'Electric Avenue'. As they sing, the stare-down falls apart.*

LAUREN. You're not meant to be making us laugh.

JAZZ. You started it.

LAUREN. You did.

JAZZ. Right, come on...

LAUREN. Come on.

> JAZZ *and* LAUREN *prepare to train and will shadow-box intermittently throughout the scene.*

JAZZ. We're supposed to be taking it serious now.

LAUREN. We are. Except for the weigh-in, I'm not doing that on the night in front of a roomful of drunks.

JAZZ. Will they be?

LAUREN. What I've heard, they're expecting an 'air-pulling, bitch-slapping, cat-fighting, comedy night.

JAZZ. Right...

LAUREN. Can't blame 'em. I would have, an' all. And it might be, who knows, ey? Who knows?

JAZZ. So are yer... d'you reckon... like, ready?

LAUREN. I'm never ready, I just do things.

JAZZ. I think too much, I think.

LAUREN. Have a kid, have another, get married, divorced, invite half the estate to see me fall flat on me face.

JAZZ. That's if I knock y'out – bang!

LAUREN. Tell Frazer-my-ex, he can come with his new bit o'stuff.

JAZZ. An' you're all right wi' that? You get on?

LAUREN. Like an 'ouse on fire yeah, now he's gone. And y'have to stay friends if you can, for the kids.

JAZZ. Course, the kids...

LAUREN. So what about you? Who's coming, your family, your friends?

JAZZ. Yeah, there might be a friend. You know, singular.

LAUREN. Are they now?

JAZZ. Cos I'd rather, you know –

LAUREN. Singular –

JAZZ. Do it wi'out all the fuss.

LAUREN. I'm assuming y'are?

JAZZ. What?

LAUREN. Singular. Cos I've not seen nobody coming or going.

JAZZ. No. I mean yeah-yeah, I am. But that's...

LAUREN. Not seen no one at all, to be fair.

JAZZ. Well, me family, we don't... they're nice people, you know... nice house an' all that... but I've not really turned out the way they... and mates, don't have to see 'em this day an' age. And you can have mates online, can't yer, now?

LAUREN. Online?

JAZZ. From all over, on forums and Skype. In America, all sorts.

LAUREN. Oh aye?

JAZZ. You don't always find like-minded folk live next door.

LAUREN. Or maybe you do?

JAZZ. I don't mean... yeah, I know you and me, we're like top mates now, us.

LAUREN. I'd never have known you were into that.

JAZZ. What?

LAUREN. Y'dark horse, I'd never have known...

LAUREN is looking at JAZZ in a new light.

JAZZ. No... cos I'm not really someone who talks about stuff like... I just find it hard to find words what... cos thoughts are thoughts, aren't they and feelings are feelings but when you start trying to say 'em out loud, I get sorta blocked in me chest here an' then... then... bur' online.

LAUREN. I know, mate.

JAZZ. On webcam, feels... safer... somehow.

LAUREN. I met Frazer when I were sixteen.

JAZZ. Sixteen...

LAUREN. Ten years, that's all I knew: him. Being Wi' Him. What he liked, I liked; what he thought, I thought; what he asked for, I did. And I'm no shrinking violent, I just got...

JAZZ. Violet.

LAUREN. What is?

JAZZ. Shrinking violet. You know, like the flower?

LAUREN. Is it?

JAZZ. Yeah.

Beat.

LAUREN. God, I'm thick.

JAZZ. You're not. And you just got…

LAUREN. Stuck, Jazz. Superglued.

JAZZ. How?

LAUREN. Same way me mum did. Pregnant at seventeen, nineteen, twenty-one accidentally, one more. We get moved to a maisonette and I'm over the moon cos there's somewhere to hang out me washing.

JAZZ. Wi' four kids, you need it.

LAUREN. That's nor' all you need but you just have to push them thoughts down… y'have to. And Frazer, he did an' all, to be fair. Gotta full-time job, worked hard. Got his bricklaying qualification and that got him contracts down London.

JAZZ. London…

LAUREN. Cos the money's so good. And he finds out he likes it, an' all. Likes staying away cos it's bedlam at home wi' the kids, and us fighting all time. So we split. Seven years ago, best thing all round. And then when they offered him Azerbaijan…

JAZZ. Where's that?

LAUREN. That's whar' I said. But we decided the boys'd have more if he went. And he's back once a month now, he stays at his mum's, so…

JAZZ. That's good.

LAUREN. Four years he's been out there. Building 'em hospitals, houses and schools. He's done well.

JAZZ. You don't miss him, then?

LAUREN. Not got the time.

JAZZ. You don't miss having someone around?

LAUREN. Didn't at first. Then it were summat I shoved to the back of the drawer wi' me size-ten pants. And then, finally, last year, I came here to Weight Watchers, thirteen-stone-six. Then Bums and Tums, down to ten.

JAZZ. Well done.

LAUREN. And now here I am, doing this. And the rest. If I'm brave enough.

JAZZ. Course y'are. You're maroon.

LAUREN. An' can you keep a secret?

Beat.

JAZZ. Yeah.

LAUREN. I mean properly… totally…

JAZZ. Yes. What?

LAUREN. That site I signed up to…

JAZZ. What about it?

LAUREN. Well, it's like what you…

JAZZ. What?

LAUREN. It's like you've just told us.

JAZZ. What have I told yer?

LAUREN. It's Mates Online… like-minded… Men.

JAZZ. Men?

LAUREN. Or whatever you're…

JAZZ. Right… I see… right…

LAUREN. You're okay wi' this, aren't yer?

JAZZ. Yeah, yeah.

LAUREN. Cos if I don't say it to someone, I think I'll go pop.

JAZZ. I'm totally fine.

LAUREN. First time I went on, I couldn't believe it, they just look like ordinary blokes…

JAZZ. But…

LAUREN. But then they start messaging you. Wi' questions and compliments, cheeky suggestions and more. Till I'm messaging six of 'em all at once. Talking to him, him and him until it's like, 'Who have I just said *that* to?' And Jazz, it gets you as horny as hell.

JAZZ. I bet.

LAUREN. On Friday, this one lad, he sends us a photo from work.

JAZZ. What does he do?

LAUREN. Wanks for a living, I reckon.

JAZZ. Lauren!

LAUREN. But it's hilarious, in't it? The fact that they do it and don't think we'll laugh.

JAZZ. You deleted it though?

LAUREN. I did once I'd sent him one back.

JAZZ. You what?

LAUREN. S'all right, they don't know us. They don't know me name or the place where I live.

JAZZ. How many more have yer…

LAUREN. One or two. Why not, wi' me new-found confidence.

JAZZ. Haven't you heard of revenge porn?

LAUREN. I'm not sending mugshots, you get me?

Beat.

JAZZ. I see.

Beat.

LAUREN. What's up?

JAZZ. Nowt.

LAUREN. Jazz?

JAZZ. Nothing, I'm just…

LAUREN. What?

JAZZ. I'm thinking, that's all.

LAUREN. Oh, come on, you do it, an' all?

JAZZ. When?

LAUREN. You said you're like-minded. You're not?

JAZZ. Not in the way you, mate... no.

Beat.

LAUREN. Do you think I'm a slag?

JAZZ. No.

LAUREN. You do, I can see on your face.

JAZZ. No way.

LAUREN. In your eyes.

JAZZ. Nor' at all.

LAUREN. And it's what you'd expect from a lass like me, ey? Dirty house, dirty mind.

JAZZ. Your house in't dirty. It's homely and friendly and full o'yer family an' laughing an' chatter an' –

LAUREN. But it's nor' always chatter you want, is it?

Beat.

JAZZ. No.

LAUREN. And there's a fella in Scunny. Kris wi' a K. We've been on WhatsApp. Turns out he's a courier.

JAZZ. What kind of –

LAUREN. And, if I want, he says he'll drop in. Wi' a package.

JAZZ. When?

LAUREN. Next Monday morning when kids are at school.

JAZZ. What time?

LAUREN. Half-nine.

JAZZ. So he won't even buy you a drink?

LAUREN. I don't wanna drink. I don't wanna feel that you have to have sex cos he's bought you three rum and Cokes.

JAZZ. I don't mean –

LAUREN. Cos I've been there, done that, too many times wi' too many lads from round here. But this way… this way, I set it up. I select. I say when and where, I choose what I wanna do and who with. And if I wanna be like a bloke, then…

JAZZ. Is that what you think a bloke is?

LAUREN. All I'm saying my body's mine now. It's mine. It's me in control.

JAZZ. But what if he's not what he says he is? What if you're tied up and slung in the back of his van, have you thought of that?

LAUREN. I think of it every day, mate, I'm a woman. But if they get lairy, I'll lamp 'em. I'd flatten 'em now, wouldn't I?

LAUREN *throws a playful shadow-punch at* JAZZ.

JAZZ. I don't want to see you get hurt.

LAUREN. You better not say that on Friday, I want a fair fight.

LAUREN *jabs again.*

JAZZ. I don't wanna hit yer. I wanna protect yer.

LAUREN. Protect me?

LAUREN *stops shadow-punching.*

JAZZ. Forget it, forget I said owt.

LAUREN. Why?

JAZZ. Cut, rewind, erase.

LAUREN. Why do I need…

JAZZ. You don't but…

LAUREN. But what?

JAZZ. But all right, if that's what you've gotta do, wanna do...
then... I'll be there, I'll be watching. Nor actually watching –

LAUREN. Well, no –

JAZZ. I'll just... I'll just make sure you're safe.

Beat.

LAUREN. No one's ever said that to me, Jazz.

JAZZ. No one's ever... from first day I got here, you've been...
an' then coming here, I feel... I feel like I can be more
myself wi' you... openly, honestly... I... and...

LAUREN *catches sight of the time.*

LAUREN. Shit, the kids!

JAZZ. What?

LAUREN. I'm picking 'em up, or I'm meant to be.

LAUREN *gathers her stuff, quickly.*

JAZZ. Sorry, sorry!

LAUREN. S'not your fault, you div.

JAZZ. I know bur' I'm sorry I...

LAUREN. Look, I've gotta lasagne defrosting. Come round
tonight and we'll chat.

JAZZ. 'Bout what?

LAUREN. Life, love and the universe, ey? And who might be
out there for you. Cos there's gotta be someone, there must be.

Exit LAUREN, running.

JAZZ. There is.

Scene Five

JAZZ begins to train hard. Alone, the routine brings a physical release for feelings as yet unspoken. Through boxing, the maleness in JAZZ's soul finds a natural expression.

Scene Six

Thursday. Cross-fade to ANETA, cleaning the floor. She goes through the motions but her mind is elsewhere. She finds herself moving around and around in ever-decreasing circles. She puts the mop down and goes to the boxing gloves, but as she picks them up, she finds no answers or comfort.

ANETA. What are you doing here, Aneta?

> GRACE *comes in for training: focused, sharp, a girl on a mission.*

GRACE. Y'what?

ANETA. Why am I here?

GRACE. Cos it's one day to Fight Night.

ANETA. It's a rhetorical question. I think.

GRACE. A what?

ANETA. It does not require a response.

GRACE. You know more English than I do.

ANETA. Don't be ridiculous.

GRACE. See?

ANETA. I can thread the needle. Doesn't mean I can mend what's...

GRACE. I don't even know what you mean half the time.

ANETA. I'm not sure I do any more.

GRACE. You sound like the Queen.

ANETA. Do I?

GRACE. You do.

GRACE *pulls on her gloves, preparing to spar.*

ANETA. You know, when I came here with Iga – ten years ago
– I thought England was Houses of Parliament, Buckingham
Palace… very naive.

GRACE. They're none of them in Hull.

ANETA. I came here for Iga. I'd work so she could study and
find a good job and have choice. Real choice. But then, of
course, came the crash.

GRACE. You had a crash?

ANETA. Financial.

GRACE. Dunno about that.

ANETA. It took us all down and still, here I am. Fighting to
stay in a cleaning job. Literally fighting.

GRACE. Why don't you go home, then?

ANETA. Oh, is that how you voted?

GRACE. Vote, me?

ANETA. Grace, women died for the right –

GRACE. But it's nowt to me, is it? Europe an' that.

ANETA. It's only your future.

GRACE. When am I gonna go there?

GRACE *gets on with her warm-up.*

ANETA. Iga was eight when we came to this country. I'd be
taking her home to a foreign land.

GRACE. Won't make no difference to her.

ANETA. Why?

GRACE. She don't go out, does she?

ANETA. How do you know?

GRACE. Just do.

ANETA. Sorry, how do you know that my daughter...

GRACE. An' I was at school wi' her, weren't I? Not in her class but...

ANETA. But what?

GRACE. I remember a girl called... what?

ANETA. Iga?

GRACE. I-gaga. Well, that's what they called her.

ANETA. I-gaga?

GRACE. Yeah. Cos she's a bit...

ANETA. What?

GRACE. You know...

ANETA. I'm not sure I do.

GRACE. You must do, you live wi' her.

ANETA. Tell me?

GRACE. Are we training or what?

ANETA. Grace? What else did they call her at school?

GRACE. It were ages ago, all that.

ANETA. What did they do?

GRACE. How do I know? I stopped going at fourteen, the Head 'ad it in for me. Tell yer, if I saw her now...

As GRACE *swings her fist,* BARBARA *appears. She starts to shadow-box, but with* GRACE, *it's as if she's needling and provoking her.* GRACE *tries to jab back but she becomes increasingly wrong-footed by* BARBARA.

ANETA. Did you know she was punched in the face by a girl there?

GRACE. Who weren't?

ANETA. Had her head banged on a table repeatedly? Called a geek and a creep and made fun of because she liked school, she liked studying, reading and writing and –

GRACE. That's how it was.

ANETA. She thinks those girls are still out there, Grace. If she goes to the shop or to college, she thinks they'll be there on the corner and guess what? They probably will.

GRACE. Just tell her forget it.

ANETA. Forget she was bullied so badly –

GRACE. She brung it on, didn't she?

Beat.

ANETA. And how do you know?

Beat.

GRACE. Cos she didn't... she wasn't... and what are you asking me now for? It were years ago and we've got training to –

ANETA. Was it you? Were you part of the gang? Were you one of those feral girls –

GRACE. No!

ANETA. Then how come you know so much, huh?

GRACE. I don't! I don't know nothing, do I?

GRACE *turns and throws punches into the air. As she does,* ANETA *takes a canvas roll from her bag.*

ANETA. Iga learned two things at school.

GRACE. Two more than I did.

ANETA. Fear and shame.

GRACE. You having a laugh?

ANETA. But as you say, I learned English: the sacred-profane mother tongue that I wanted to speak to perfection.

GRACE. Shut up now.

ANETA. And from my own mother, I learned to cook.

GRACE. Big wow.

ANETA. Beautiful *bigos*, gorgeous *gołąbki*. And oh, her *pierogi*. You ever tried *pierogi*?

GRACE. Sounds gross.

ANETA. And you know what? I still have my grandmother's knife.

ANETA *unrolls a kitchen knife and takes it out.*

GRACE. What you –

ANETA. It has no value, of course. Except to me.

GRACE. Put it away now.

ANETA. And to my daughter.

GRACE. If Taylor sees us wi' that.

ANETA. She values it so much, she hid it under her pillow last night.

GRACE. What you telling me for?

ANETA. Cos you can tell me what put it there?

GRACE. She did.

ANETA. Was it fear, Grace? Or shame?

ANETA *offers* GRACE *the knife.* BARBARA *stops. Now she's watching* GRACE, *as if willing her towards the truth.*

GRACE. What?

ANETA. Take it.

GRACE. No.

ANETA. Take. It.

GRACE *does, she is given no choice.*

GRACE. Now what?

ANETA. Take it away… take it anywhere… I can't handle it, any of it any more, I…

Enter NORA.

NORA. What's all this commotion –

ANETA. Take it!

The sight of GRACE *with the knife stops* NORA *dead.*

NORA. What's this?

GRACE. It's not what you think.

NORA. Oh, really?

GRACE (*to* ANETA). Tell her.

NORA. Put it down.

GRACE. I'm not.

GRACE *moves across the room with the knife in her hand.* NORA *has to move out of her path, and quickly.*

NORA. Put it down or I'm calling the police.

GRACE. Call 'em. I'm gone.

GRACE *puts the knife down. As she goes out,* GRACE *runs into* LAUREN.

LAUREN. Oi, road-hog!

What's up wi' her?

NORA. What happened?

ANETA. It's nothing…

NORA. Nothing?

ANETA. It's done…

LAUREN. Where's Jazz? I called for her on the way in but –

NORA. She's a bad 'un, I said from the start.

ANETA. Nora, I need to go home.

LAUREN. Why? What's wrong?

ANETA. It's personal.

LAUREN. Yeah, what?

ANETA. I need to go home and stay there till all this is over.

NORA. Aneta, why?

ANETA. Cos if I get up there with Grace, I will kill her.

NORA. Come on, you're not that good.

ANETA. I need to go.

> *As* ANETA *starts to gather her stuff,* TAYLOR *enters, with a copy of the* Hull Daily Mail.

TAYLOR. Nora –

NORA. You can't. You're committed.

ANETA. Yes, to an asylum.

TAYLOR. Can I have a word, please?

NORA. Not –

TAYLOR. Now!

> NORA *turns to* TAYLOR.

NORA. 'Bout what?

TAYLOR. Page five of the *Hull Daily Mail*.

NORA. Oh, is it in?

LAUREN. What?

NORA. Just a thing about Friday.

LAUREN. 'Bout us?

TAYLOR. 'Tis, yeah.

NORA. Well, go on. Read it.

> TAYLOR *turns to page five.* BARBARA *listens intently.*

TAYLOR. 'For weeks, they've been skipping, sparring and punching. Now four local girls are pulling on the gloves for a major fundraiser.'

LAUREN. 'Major'?

TAYLOR. 'The Six Bells Gala Fight Night sees the pub's Women's Boxing Club ducking and diving to raise funds for vital community projects.'

NORA. Read on.

TAYLOR. 'Landlady Nora Moore, forty-six – '

LAUREN. Now you're having a laugh.

TAYLOR. 'Said: "The girls are as good as the lads in the ring. They can't wait to go head-to-head with each other and show off their skills."'

ANETA. Okay...

TAYLOR. 'Skills they've learned from a former Brit boxer who's come back to show 'em the ropes.'

NORA. Ey?

TAYLOR. '"Taylor Flint is a legend in Hull,"' says Nora.'

NORA. Oh, I never...

TAYLOR. 'She just wants to give back into the community that gave her so much.'

NORA. Nor' on the record. I told him, I said...

TAYLOR. 'And if you wanna see her in action, come down on Friday night.'

NORA. I said 'surprise guest', that's all.

TAYLOR *throws down the paper.*

BARBARA. Don't read your press. Measure it.

LAUREN. But it's true, y'are a legend.

TAYLOR. No, I'm an ex-con who's just breached her terms of her licence.

NORA. Taylor –

TAYLOR. Not her *boxing* licence, that's long gone. Her parole.

ANETA. How?

TAYLOR. By missing me meeting today cos of this.

NORA. That were a stupid thing to do.

TAYLOR. What's stupid is me gettin' sucked into your...

Enter JAZZ, *running.*

JAZZ. I've just seen Grace...

TAYLOR. We'll have *The Sun* at the door next, we'll...

JAZZ. She's outside.

TAYLOR. Go to jail –

JAZZ. By the bins.

TAYLOR. Go directly to jail –

JAZZ. Gasping –

TAYLOR. Do not pass 'Go' –

JAZZ. She says her inhaler's in here.

JAZZ and LAUREN *search for* GRACE*'s inhaler.*

NORA. Taylor, chillax.

TAYLOR. 'Chillax'? When I told yer –

NORA. You've told me a lot of things, gal.

JAZZ. Go get her, Aneta.

ANETA. No.

JAZZ. Go!

Exit ANETA.

TAYLOR. I told you exhibition match, word-of-mouth only.

NORA. I've gotta sell tickets, that's not enough.

TAYLOR. Not my problem.

NORA. I need this to be an event.

TAYLOR. How? By putting me back inside?

NORA. Have they said that?

TAYLOR. Not yet but it's only a matter of time.

LAUREN. Got it.

Enter ANETA, *helping* GRACE.

ANETA. She'd followed you in.

GRACE. Quick...

LAUREN. Here.

GRACE *takes the inhaler and breathes in.*

NORA. Well, if they try it, we'll fight it, we'll –

TAYLOR. No one's fighting. That's it. No exhibition, no Fight Night, no fight.

JAZZ. What d'you mean?

TAYLOR. It's over. Everything. Over and done.

LAUREN. Now, hang on! We've worked for this, Taylor.

JAZZ. We're primed.

TAYLOR. Well, tough.

LAUREN. Come on, Tay.

TAYLOR. Cos I'm not going back. I mean it, I tell yer, I can't be locked up in there on my own. I can't do it, I can't, I can't...

LAUREN. Taylor...

TAYLOR. Don't. Don't look at me, don't...

NORA. Taylor –

TAYLOR. Please don't...

Beat.

LAUREN. Taylor, mate? You know we know, don't yer?

Beat.

TAYLOR. Know what?

LAUREN. We know you got drunk and got into a fight in a club. Wi' a bloke who were winding y'up, saying 'who do you think y'are' an' all that.

We know you caned him an' threw him downstairs and got three years for your trouble.

TAYLOR. I rose to the bait.

LAUREN. And we all know that shit happens, mate. To all of us, to the best of us.

JAZZ. Does.

ANETA. Every day.

LAUREN. And you're home now. It's over.

NORA's mobile rings.

TAYLOR. See? That's them on the phone, that's probation, they know where I am an' –

ANETA. Just breathe, Taylor.

JAZZ. Use the fear. Work with it.

TAYLOR. Now?

NORA's mobile is insistently ringing. ANETA picks it up and looks at the display.

ANETA. Theresa May?

NORA. Leave it.

The call goes to voicemail, leaving a charged silence.

ANETA. She's gone.

NORA's mobile rings again.

TAYLOR. I'm gone, I'm finished, I'm done.

NORA. Taylor!

ANETA. Right, enough!

ANETA picks up the phone.

The Six Bells? No, I'm sorry. She's in a meeting at present.

TAYLOR. She knows, she knows.

NORA. Put her on speaker.

ANETA. This is Aneta, the Hygiene Manager. If I can give her a message or...

NORA. Put her on speaker to calm her.

ANETA puts the phone on to speaker. We hear THERESA MAY FROM THE BREWERY loud and clear. BARBARA is in the shadows, listening too.

THERESA (*voice-over*). Well, perhaps you can answer my question.

ANETA. I'll try, madame, yes.

THERESA (*voice-over*). It's been brought to our attention The Six Bells has a 'Fight Night' occurring.

ANETA. Oh, yes?

THERESA (*voice-over*). Tomorrow night.

ANETA. Right...

THERESA (*voice-over*). A Women's Fight Night.

Everyone is listening intently, including GRACE.

NORA. S'all right, Tay... s'all right...

ANETA. And how do you know about this?

TAYLOR. See?

THERESA (*voice-over*). The *Hull Daily Mail*. So my question to you is simply this: does Mrs Cooke have a licence?

ANETA. As far as I know, this is a licensed premises. She can have music and sports an' all sorts. Up to midnight.

THERESA (*voice-over*). But you may not know, Anita, that boxing, wrestling and mixed martial-arts contests, exhibitions and displays qualify as Regulated Entertainment and thus require their own application.

ANETA. Okay.

THERESA (*voice-over*). To the local authority.

ANETA. You mean the council?

THERESA (*voice-over*). Has this application been made?

ANETA *looks at* NORA, *who raises her eyebrows.*

ANETA. I will ask Mrs Cooke to contact you.

THERESA (*voice-over*). As soon as she can, please.

ANETA. I will tell her. ASAP.

THERESA (*voice-over*). And perhaps you'll also remind her that holding an unlicensed event would put her in breach of her tenancy.

ANETA. I'm sure she will be aware of that, thank you –

THERESA (*voice-over*). And may I ask you something, Anita?

ANETA. Aneta.

THERESA (*voice-over*). Do you know Nora well?

ANETA *looks at* NORA.

ANETA. Yes. Very well.

THERESA (*voice-over*). Then may I speak to you in more of a personal…

ANETA. Yes. Please do. Madame.

THERESA (*voice-over*). We're concerned here… we've been concerned for a while that she's possibly losing a little…

ANETA. Money? Well, times are tough.

THERESA (*voice-over*). And she hasn't quite grasped the commercial reality of… in the current climate… and as

a result, she's making what we feel are ill-informed,
ill-advised...

ANETA. Okay...

THERESA (*voice-over*). But more than that... in terms of...
we're concerned that she's... not very well.

ANETA. She needs a hip replacement, we all know that.

THERESA (*voice-over*). Not just her mobility, although
that's... not very well in herself.

ANETA. Oh?

THERESA (*voice-over*). Now, I've a great deal of time for Old
Nora. She's a battler, she's Hull through and through. But.
In recent months, we've detected an edge... a resistance...

ANETA. Resistance is good.

THERESA (*voice-over*). A rather irrational loss of perspective
that's making us think that perhaps... she might need some
help.

ANETA. Aren't you there to help her, madame?

THERESA (*voice-over*). We can help if Mrs Cooke lets us. But
if she won't, if she can't... if she wants to see girls knocking
seven bells out of each other –

ANETA. Six Bells.

THERESA (*voice-over*). It's all very laudable wanting to 'save
the community' but when you believe it's your mission in
life, and that 'only you' can –

ANETA. I disagree.

Silence falls in the room and on the line.

Hello?

THERESA (*voice-over*). The Six Bells is a business, Anita.

ANETA. Aneta.

THERESA (*voice-over*). Not a charity, not a community centre and certainly not a venue where unlicensed, frankly illicit, activities will be allowed to take place in our name. Understand?

ANETA. I hear you, Theresa.

THERESA (*voice-over*). My name is –

ANETA *ends the call. The silence hangs heavy.*

NORA. And for the record... my name is Nora Anne Cooke. Née Manston. Hessle Road girl. Married twenty-eight years to Davy, skipper on' *Susie May*. Who worked and saved so his son wouldn't have to do as he done. And he didn't. He left us September 16th 1993. Aged seventeen. Overdose. Heroin.

GRACE. I didn't know.

NORA. Now you do.

ANETA. Aneta Śląska. Born Warsaw. Long road, there to here. But I come for my daughter and... and I will never forsake her.

LAUREN. Lauren Lee. I dunno... Hull Forever.

JAZZ. Jazz. None of th'above. Still, y'know... working it out. What I am. But... but I know what I'm not... and I know things are changing and...

LAUREN. Go on.

JAZZ. It's hard to...

LAUREN. Always is... moment of truth.

JAZZ. And the truth is, I'm... transitioning.

LAUREN. Right...

JAZZ. From this to... to the person I am an' I've always been, deep down inside. And if it means I can't do it, you know... the fight... cos it's kind-of unfair cos the class is for... I shoulda come clean, said right from the start but –

LAUREN. Oh, you're doing it, mate.

JAZZ. But it weren't till I came and came out of myself that I, like, found my...

LAUREN. You don't get out of it that easy – maroon.

JAZZ. You're maroon.

GRACE. I'm Grace Idlewell. Didn't ask to be born but I was, so... (*To* ANETA.) I'll talk to her.

ANETA. Iga.

GRACE. I'll go round and tell her I did it to her, cos they did it to me.

ANETA. You will?

GRACE. If you'll do us a dinner. Peer...

ANETA. *Pierogi.*

GRACE. An' cos we're all, like... 'transitioning'... aren't we? Or trying to.

NORA. Taylor?

The women wait for TAYLOR*'s response. As she does,* BARBARA *appears in her eyeline.* TAYLOR *addresses her story to her.*

TAYLOR. When... when I started all this, I were the only one. Me on me own or I thought I was. No other girls in the gym. So I were sparring wi' lads.

BARBARA. Lads who don't wanna hit yer.

TAYLOR. Not so you know you'd been hit.

BARBARA. They're embarrassed.

TAYLOR. Their ego hurts more when they're punched by a girl, way more. But I stuck at it... kept going, I had to...

BARBARA. I had to...

TAYLOR. Till...

GRACE. Till?

BARBARA *steps back for* TAYLOR *to continue. She now talks to the class.*

TAYLOR. Till one lad who's sent in to spar wi' me, full three stone heavier... dancing round, tapping at me, all of that... till I land a beautiful shot on his nose. And finally, instinct kicks in and he floors us.

LAUREN. No way?

TAYLOR. I'm up on me feet then I'm kissing the canvas. Shocked to the core. Laughing... angry... outraged... panicked... ashamed.

JAZZ. Why ashamed?

TAYLOR. It's one thought right after the other: bang, bang, bang, bang, bang, bang, bang. I'm reeling and spinning but then... then I see clear as day.

JAZZ. What?

TAYLOR. That I'm not a girl in the ring. Not a guy. I'm animal. Fight or flight, primal, it's pure, it's like nothing else. You're...

BARBARA *unflinchingly meets* TAYLOR*'s gaze.*

BARBARA. Alive.

TAYLOR. And you feel like anything's possible.

LAUREN *turns to the group.*

LAUREN. Fight or flight?

JAZZ/GRACE/ANETA. Fight.

Scene Seven

Boxing ring. The space is defined by light. From dark corners come the sounds of a full house: male and female, young and old, drunk and sober. Everyone's up for a good time but there's a hint of menace in the air. The crowd begin to feel dangerously close.

Enter LAUREN, JAZZ, ANETA *and* GRACE. *They are wearing a mix of* TAYLOR*'s and Don Shaw's gear. They take a corner each and pull on their headguards.*

NORA *takes centre-stage, with a microphone, echoing the fairground barker of the opening scene.*

NORA. Ladies and gentlemen! In a charity spectacular, The Six Bells presents one of the most inspirational entertainments ever to be seen in East Yorkshire. You're here tonight to see the very best and brightest and bravest that Hull has to offer! A Fight Night like no other!

Cheers and wolf-whistles, especially when group names are called.

We've got Weight Watchers in! Knitters and Natterers! Bums and Tums! Alpha! So without further ado... here they are... in the footsteps of the great Barbara Buttrick... our fighting foursome...

Cheers from the crowd.

I bring you... from Cedar Court, 'All That' Jazz!

JAZZ *nods to a muted yet supportive reaction.*

Also from Cedar Court, Lauren 'What Y'Looking At' Lee!

LAUREN *salutes the partisan crowd.*

From Beech Ave, Aneta 'Up the Pole' Śląska.

ANETA *gives a strangely flamboyant bow.*

And from Sycamore Way... she's banned, yes banned from The Six Bells but on special licence, I give you Grace 'Gobshite' Idlewell!

GRACE *raises her fist to cheers, boos and heckles.*

And our referee for tonight needs no introduction... she's a Hull boxing legend... she's our very own Taaaaylor Fliiiiint!

TAYLOR *steps out to a massive cheer. She gestures for the four girls to come to her.*

TAYLOR. Number-one thing to remember now: breathe. Cos breathing is pace. You fight t'your breath, you fight t'your pace. And you breathe when *you* breathe, got it? Not when she lets you cos that way, you stay in control. You're aggressive not angry, you don't fight the fear and you breathe.

LAUREN. Breathe.

ANETA. Breathe.

JAZZ. Breathe.

GRACE. Breathe.

TAYLOR. Two rounds. Two minutes.

LAUREN. I can piss longer than that.

TAYLOR. S'all down to you now. You're it, the one and only. You've trained hard and now, here, tonight... you step up and claim your reward, so... no holding, no hitting on the break, no illegal punches, no low blows. Protect yourselves at all times. If I give the eight-count, go to a neutral corner and stay there till I give the word, you got me?

GRACE. Yep –

LAUREN. Sure –

JAZZ. Right –

ANETA. Yes.

TAYLOR. Touch gloves.

The fighters touch gloves.

Corners.

The crowd gives a massive and emotionally charged cheer which carries the four back to their corners.

NORA *rings the bell.*

NORA. Round One.

Two simultaneous fights begin: LAUREN *versus* JAZZ *and*
ANETA *versus* GRACE. *The couples move around their
opponents and each another and the timing of the rounds are
compressed into a montage.*

*Round One is messy and anarchic. No one has the upper
hand.* TAYLOR *is the fulcrum around which it revolves. The
choreography brings certain moments to the foreground but
as the bell rings, there is no clear front-runner.*

What a night! What a fight! Could you call it? Can you, sir?
No way!

The four briefly retreat to their corners. TAYLOR *goes to one
with a sponge and a bucket, and a word of encouragement we
don't hear.*

NORA *rings the bell.*

Seconds out... Round Two.

The four re-enter the ring. As Round Two progresses,
LAUREN *and* GRACE *pile on the pressure. The anarchic
spirit intensifies.* LAUREN *and* GRACE *surge ahead in the
final moments, landing punches which make* ANETA *and*
JAZZ *stumble and fall.*

NORA *rings the bell.*

And the winner is...

TAYLOR. Lauren! Grace!

TAYLOR *lifts their fists.* LAUREN *and* GRACE *take their
applause. All four then return to their corners.*

NORA. And now, friends – The Final!

LAUREN. What final?

NORA. Fighting for The Six Bells Belt: Lauren Lee and Grace
Idlewell!

GRACE. You ready? You ready!

LAUREN. No.

> LAUREN *and* GRACE *come out of their corners and square up to one another.* TAYLOR *moves in and around them as they fight. The temperature is rising to boiling point.*

> LAUREN *has the edge, then* GRACE, *then* LAUREN. *They are fighting with a rising sense of liberation. They are battling one another yet rising and falling together. The momentum builds into a thrilling routine. The crowd are going wild. In the intense heat of the moment,* GRACE *swings her fist. She misses* LAUREN *but hits* TAYLOR *square in the face. The crowd gasp as* TAYLOR *stumbles and hits the deck.*

> TAYLOR *loses consciousness. A surreal silence falls. Our focus shifts to* TAYLOR's *punch-drunk perspective. From the silence comes a heartbeat, heavy breathing and then, a count: distance at first, then louder.*

COUNT. Three... four... five... six...

> TAYLOR *looks up through the hazy light to see* BARBARA *prowling the ring, mid-fight, waiting for the knockout 'ten'.*

Seven... eight... nine...

> TAYLOR *springs to her feet.* BARBARA *turns. The fight isn't over yet.*

> TAYLOR *and* BARBARA *fight with skill and passion, in a blood-and-glory bout, an almighty clash of faith, commitment and courage. The spirit of Hull heroines past and present is embodied in their struggle.* NORA *gives a fragmented and surreal commentary.*

NORA. In the first officially sanctioned Women's World Boxing Championship – Little Barbara, quick as a cat, peppered her foe with lightning lefts to the head and face – followed through with right-hand shots to the body – sharp left jab – grim determination – forced the fight with her outclassed opponent – won for herself the World's Women's

Bantamweight Championship – after TEN YEARS of professional fighting – Won thirty, drew one, lost one and twelve knockouts!!

BARBARA *punches* TAYLOR *and she hits the canvas. As she falls, we snap back to reality. The chants give way to the cries of the group.*

NORA. Taylor!

JAZZ. Taylor!

GRACE. Sorry, sorry, sorry –

LAUREN. Taylor, mate?

GRACE. Come on, Taylor. Get up, get up!

TAYLOR *allows the women to lift her up.*

TAYLOR. I am, I am.

NORA. Y'all right, gal?

TAYLOR. Yeah-yeah.

NORA. You sure now?

GRACE. You sure?

TAYLOR *looks around but* BARBARA *is gone. The crowd are chanting, keeping the temperature at boiling point.*

TAYLOR. I'm good, yeah… yeah… I'm fantastic!

GRACE. Y'are?

TAYLOR. And so was that.

GRACE. What?

TAYLOR *shadows* GRACE'*s punch.*

TAYLOR. You've got it, Grace.

GRACE. Me?

TAYLOR. You've got it.

GRACE. So will you work wi' us, train us, tell us everything you know, so… Taylor, will yer?

NORA (*to the crowd*). Down but nor' out. Never out!

CROWD. Taylor Flint, Taylor Flint, Taylor Flint!

NORA. Go on, talk to 'em. Tell 'em.

TAYLOR. What?

NORA *shoves the microphone in her hand.*

NORA. Tell 'em.

TAYLOR *can barely speak from exhaustion but the crowd carry her through.*

TAYLOR. Heart. Faith. Spirit. Strength. Our city – our culture – our home – my home – my homies – fast hands, fast feet, quick minds, see? And this… this is who we are… this energy, this nuclear energy… we're mighty, us… each and every one of us… Mighty Atoms!

GRACE, LAUREN, ANETA *and* JAZZ *face the audience: headguards off, battered and bloodied but not beaten. They take hold of another's wrist and raise their arms.*

ALL. Mighty Atoms!

Hull Truck Theatre

Hull Truck Theatre is dedicated to delivering exceptional theatre for a diverse audience, including those encountering it for the first time.

As part of our Hull UK City of Culture 2017 programme we're producing work on an unprecedented scale, with some of the largest cast sizes ever to grace our stages. We are thrilled to be working with an exceptional range of internationally renowned artists and companies, commissioning writers to produce world premieres right here in Hull, and working with local people to tell their own unique stories.

We see culture as a powerful regenerative tool for our city, enabling it to meet its ambitions and commitment to overcoming social and economic challenges. We are a pioneering theatre with a contemporary northern voice, locally rooted and global in outlook, inspiring artists, exciting audiences and supporting communities to reach their greatest potential.

Through our work with schools and with the community, we help to raise aspirations and give life-changing creative opportunities to thousands of young people, disabled groups and adults.

'We believe that everyone has the right to enjoy and be enriched by high-quality artistic work that is culturally relevant to people and place, in a positive and welcoming environment. We aim to be a thriving creative organisation that tells extraordinary human stories, offering fresh and imaginative perspectives on the world.'

Mark Babych, Artistic Director

Artistic Director Mark Babych
Executive Director Janthi Mills-Ward

Board
Alan Dix (Chair)
Alan Kirkman (Vice-Chair)
Sophie Buckley
Paul Clay
Steve Gallant
David Gemmell OBE
Jenni Grainger
Carol Hancock
David Hilton
Anthony McReavy
Cllr Helene O'Mullane
Dawn Walton

Hull Truck Theatre
50 Ferensway
Hull
HU2 8LB
www.hulltruck.co.uk

Hull Truck Theatre gratefully acknowledges funding from:

Hull Truck Theatre History

Hull Truck Theatre tells powerful human stories that resonate with our times.

We have been creating exciting performances for over forty-five years, starting with a group of friends making theatre in the back of a truck, to a venue on Spring Street, to our purpose-built home on Ferensway.

The company began in 1972 after director Mike Bradwell placed a magazine advert reading 'half-formed theatre company seeks other half'. Various artists responded, moved to Hull and began devising their own plays – Hull Truck Theatre was born. An anarchic spirit and a passion for telling stories were at the heart of the company from the very beginning and brought our performances to national attention.

In the 1980s, John Godber took the helm. We moved to our first permanent building, a renovated church hall on Hull's Spring Street, creating a stream of popular hits which toured to great acclaim.

In 2012, we celebrated our fortieth anniversary by moving into a new home on Ferensway, and the following year Artistic Director Mark Babych joined to lead the company on the next stage of our journey.

We create exceptional drama which builds on traditions laid down by writers including Anthony Minghella and Alan Plater, as well as creating new work with artists such as Amanda Whittington, Tom Wells, Tanika Gupta and Bryony Lavery. We make work with local people, programme the very best in live performance, and build partnerships with others to create a vibrant and dynamic cultural hub for Hull that is inspiring, creative and welcoming.

Hull UK City of Culture 2017

The story so far…

When in 2013 it was announced that Hull was to be UK City of Culture 2017, the city erupted with huge excitement.

It's an award given every four years to a city that demonstrates the belief in the transformative power of culture. Here was an unprecedented opportunity to put Hull on the map and to help build a legacy, positioning it as a place to live, visit, study and invest in.

Culture Company (Hull 2017), established to deliver on that promise, set out to produce 365 days of great art and cultural events inspired by the city and told to the world. The ambition was to create a nationally significant event that celebrates the unique character of Hull, its people and heritage. It offers a programme that takes in every art form, from theatre and performance, to visual arts and literature, to music and film, which goes into every corner of the city, whilst showcasing it nationally.

Working with local as well as national and international artists and cultural institutions, Hull 2017 also draws on the distinctive spirit of the city and the artists, writers, directors, musicians, revolutionaries and thinkers that have made such a significant contribution to the development of art and ideas.

The positive reaction to the programme has exceeded all expectations, with Hull now being taken seriously as a cultural destination for must-see events. The theatre programme for the year is set to continue to challenge and thrill new and existing audiences in the city and beyond, and will set the standard for the quality of work to expect from Hull in the future.

www.hull2017.co.uk